THE One & Only fish and seafood Cookbook

THE One & Only fish and seafood Cookbook

All the recipes you will ever need

With a foreword by
Jenny Linford

WeldonOwen
PUBLISHING

First published in the UK by
Weldon Owen Ltd., an imprint of the Bonnier Group
The Plaza
535 King's Road
London
SW10 0SZ
www.weldonowen.co.uk
www.bonnierpublishing.com

ISBN-13: 978 1 78342 221 0

A catalogue record for this book is available from the
British Library

Printed and bound by Interak, Poland
10 9 8 7 6 5 4 3 2 1

"In the hands of an able cook,
fish can become an inexhaustible
source of perpetual delight."

Jean-Anthelme Brillat-Savarin

Contents

Foreword

By Jenny Linford

The wonderful world of fish and seafood cookery is fantastically diverse, offering something for everyone's taste. Fish and seafood can be used to create easy meals such as Italian classic spaghetti vongole or eye-catching dinner party creations with which to impress your guests, such as a roasted whole fish. There are numerous cooking techniques with which to experiment, from gently steaming to speedy deep-frying. Flavouring that goes well with fish and seafood range from Mediterranean classics such as garlic, tomatoes and fresh herbs to fragrant Asian spices or aromatic ginger. The speed at which fish and seafood cooks – a matter of minutes, even for a whole fish – makes them a fantastically quick and convenient food with which to create delicious meals.

Source well

Absolute freshness is what you want when shopping for fish and seafood. Fresh seafood has the best flavour and texture and is also the safest to eat. If you have a good fishmongers near you – use it! Experienced fishmongers do the selecting work for you, buying the best fish and seafood from their suppliers that they can. They offer advice on what to choose, how to cook it and also prepare it for you; gutting it in seconds or expertly filleting a whole fish with a few deft strokes of the knife.

Choose carefully

When choosing whole fish, signs of freshness to look for are: bright red gills and bright shiny eyes rather than dull sunken ones, and flesh that feels firm to the touch and does not give a coating of clear slime. Importantly, fresh fish should only smell faintly of the sea rather than unpleasantly 'fishy'. Squid and octopus should have a fresh, sea smell, rather than a strong odour and be bright white in colour. Having bought your fresh fish or seafood, do make sure you eat it soon, ideally on the day of purchase.

Shellfish safety

When buying live shellfish, such as mussels or clams, store them in the fridge and make sure that you cook them as soon as soon as possible after purchase. Before cooking, go through the shellfish checking that they are either tightly closed or close when tapped; if they are open or stay open, then discard them. Also discard them if the shells are chipped or broken. Rinse thoroughly under running water, scraping off any barnacles from the shells. Once cooked, the shellfish should open. If they stay closed after cooking, then discard them.

Cleaning squid

Although you can buy prepared squid, buying a whole squid and cleaning it yourself is the cheapest and freshest option. Hold the body, then firmly pull the tentacle head so that it comes away, complete with attached white entrails. Discard the beak from the centre of the tentacles. Reach into the squid cavity to pull out and discard the firm cartilage quill inside. Pull off and reserve the two fins on either side of the body. Peel the purple membrane off the body and discard the membrane. Rinse out the pouch-shaped squid body thoroughly. Cut off and reserve the tentacles, discarding the head and its entrails. The squid body, fins and tentacles are now ready to be cooked.

Deveining prawns

Large raw prawns with their shells on are best 'deveined', a process which removes the intestinal tract resembling a slender black line running along the back of the prawn. To devein a prawn, first twist off the head, then peel off the shell working from the belly side where the shell is softer. Using a small, sharp knife, make a shallow cut along the back of the prawn and use the knife or your fingers to pull out and discard the black threadlike gut. Rinse the prawn well.

Watch your timing

Because fish and seafood cook so quickly, it is very important to keep an eye on the clock when cooking it. It's all too easy to over-cook fish and seafood. Seafood such as raw prawns, shellfish or squid will cook in a matter of seconds, depending on the cooking method. When judging cooking times, it's a matter of common sense. A large fish roasted on the bone (a very flavourful way to cook it) will take longer than a fish fillet fried in a heated pan. Roasting fish, however, usually only take 15–20 minutes, depending on its size. To test whether a whole roast fish has cooked through, simply cut into the fish down onto the backbone at the thickest part. If the flesh is opaque and comes away from the bone, it's ready.

Fish pie

1. Place the potatoes in a saucepan. Add enough water to just cover the potatoes. Add a pinch of salt and bring to a boil. Reduce the heat and simmer for 10–15 minutes or until just tender. Test with a skewer to check if done.

2. Meanwhile, heat the oven to 200°C (400°F). Place the fish and milk in a saucepan. Bring to a boil. Reduce the heat and simmer, covered, for 10 minutes or until the fish flakes easily.

3. Remove the fish with a slotted spoon. Strain the milk through a sieve and reserve the liquid. Flake the fish in large chunks. Place the fish chunks in an ovenproof dish. Slice the eggs into quarters and arrange on top of the fish.

4. Melt 50g butter in a saucepan. Add the leeks and cook gently for 3 minutes or until softened. Stir in the flour and cook for another minute. Gradually stir in the milk and cook, stirring constantly, until the sauce thickens. Season with salt and pepper, then stir in the parsley. Spoon the sauce over the fish.

5. When the potatoes are cooked, drain well and return to the heat for a few seconds to discard any remaining moisture. Add 25g butter and mash well. Pipe or spoon the potato on top of the fish. Bake for 35–45 minutes or until the top is crisp and golden.

Preparation time: 30 min
Cooking time: 1 h 20 min
Serves 4

900g potatoes, peeled and chopped into chunks
450g cod or haddock, skinned
225g undyed smoked cod or haddock, skinned
600ml milk
2 hard-boiled eggs
75g butter
2 leeks, washed and sliced
75g plain flour
salt and pepper to taste
4 tbsp fresh parsley, chopped

Thai crab cakes

1. Chop the white fish into chunks and place in a food processor with the crab meat, curry paste, fish sauce and coriander. Sprinkle the cornflour over the fish and process until the mixture is finely minced.

2. Remove the fish mixture from the processor and whisk in the spring onions with enough beaten egg to bind the mixture together. Using lightly floured hands, shape the mixture into 12 small patties. Refrigerate the patties for 30 minutes.

3. Meanwhile, prepare the cucumber salad. Peel the cucumber and slice in half. Use a teaspoon to scoop out the seeds and discard them. Chop into thick slices and place them in a bowl. Add the chillies, onion and coriander leaves. Mix the sugar, vinegar, fish sauce and sesame oil together and pour it over the cucumber mixture. Toss to combine.

4. To cook the crab cakes, shallow-fry each side of the patties for 2–3 minutes until crisp and golden. Drain well and serve with the cucumber salad.

Preparation time: 20 min
  plus 30 min chilling
Cooking time: 6 min
Serves 4

Crab cakes:
175g white fish fillets, skinned
300g white crab meat
3 tbsp Thai red curry paste
2 tbsp fish sauce
1 tbsp chopped coriander leaves
3 tbsp cornflour
2 spring onions, trimmed and thinly
  sliced
1 egg, lightly whisked
oil, for shallow frying

Cucumber salad:
1 cucumber
2 red chillies, seeded and thinly
  sliced
1 small red onion, sliced
a handful of coriander leaves
15g light muscovado sugar
2 tbsp rice wine vinegar
2 tsp fish sauce
2 tsp sesame oil

Crispy fish gougons with tartare sauce

1. To make the tartare sauce: combine all the tartare sauce ingredients together. Allow to stand for at least 30 minutes for the flavours to combine.

2. To make the gougons: heat the oven to 200°C (400°F). Slice the plaice into 1cm wide strips. combine the breadcrumbs and sesame seeds. Season the flour. Dust the fish strips with the seasoned flour, then dip in the egg before coating with the sesame seed mixture. Lay on an oiled baking sheet.

3. Brush with the sunflower oil and bake in the centre of the oven for 15–20 minutes or until crisp and golden.

4. Serve with the tartare sauce.

Preparation time: 20 min
  plus 30 min infusing
Cooking time: 20 min
Serves 4

450g plaice fillets, skinned
10 tbsp dried breadcrumbs
5 tbsp sesame seeds
2 tbsp plain flour
1 egg, lightly whisked
3 tbsp sunflower oil

For the tartare sauce:
175ml mayonnaise
1 tbsp gherkins, chopped
1 tbsp capers, chopped
1 tbsp lemon juice
1 tbsp fresh parsley, chopped

Filo-wrapped king prawns with watercress sauce

Preparation time: 25 min
    plus 30 min refrigeration
Cooking time: 15 min
Serves 4

12 king prawns
2 spring onions, trimmed and finely
    chopped
1 garlic, crushed
2 tbsp lemon juice
1 tbsp olive oil
4 sheets filo pastry

For the watercress sauce:
75g watercress
2 spring onions
150ml natural yoghurt
a pinch of grated nutmeg

1. Peel the prawns, removing their heads and body shells but leaving the tail attached. Place them in a shallow non-metallic dish.

2. Combine the spring onions, garlic, lemon juice and olive oil. Pour this mixture over the prawns. Turn over to coat the prawns in the marinade and refrigerate for 30 minutes.

3. Meanwhile, make the watercress sauce. Place all the sauce ingredients in a food processor and blend to produce a creamy dip. Transfer to a serving dish and refrigerate until required.

4. Heat the oven to 190°C (375°F). Remove the prawns from the marinade. Cut the filo pastry sheets into 10cm x 20cm strips. Brush each sheet of filo pastry lightly with olive oil. Wrap each prawn in the filo pastry, leaving the tail end sticking out. Place on a greased baking sheet.

5. Bake for 15 minutes until the pastry is crisp and the prawns are well cooked. Serve with the watercress sauce as a dip.

Potted prawns

1. Chop the butter into chunks and place in a saucepan. Melt over a low heat, stirring gently. Add the spices, salt, pepper and prawns. Stir gently for 30 seconds to 1 minute, until warm. Take care not to 'cook' the prawns as they will become tough.

2. Stir in the parsley. Remove from the heat divide between 4 small ramekin dishes. Allow the butter to set, then refrigerate until required.

3. To serve, remove from the refrigerator and allow to reach room temperature (about 15–20 minutes). Serve with brown bread or toast, with a lemon wedge for squeezing and a few fresh salad leaves to garnish.

Preparation time: 15 min
  plus refrigeration
Cooking time: 5 min
Serves 4

150g butter
pinch cayenne pepper
pinch allspice
300g small peeled prawns
1 tbsp chopped fresh parsley

To serve:
sliced brown bread or toast
lemon wedges
salad leaves

Plaice meuniere

1. Wash the plaice and pat dry with kitchen paper.

2. Place the flour on a large plate and season with salt and pepper.

3. Heat the butter in a large frying pan until it begins to bubble. Dredge the fish in the seasoned flour, shaking off the excess, and place in the pan, skin-side down.

4. Cook very gently for 3–4 minutes. Carefully turn the fish and continue cooking. Scatter in the parsley and baste the fish with the butter as it finishes cooking.

5. The fish is ready when the flesh comes away from the bone easily. Garnish the fish with the lemon slices and parsley sprigs.

Preparation time: 10 min
Cooking time: 10 min
Serves 2

1 large plaice, cleaned and trimmed
100g flour
salt and pepper to taste
100g butter
2 tbsp chopped parsley, plus sprigs
   to serve
lemon slices, to serve

Pan-fried salmon with sweet potato chilli mash

1. Peel the sweet potatoes and chop into 2.5cm chunks. Place in a saucepan with just enough water to cover. Add a few drops of lemon juice. Bring to the boil, add a little salt and simmer for 5–10 minutes or until tender.

2. In a small pan, melt the butter, add the chilli and garlic and cook gently for 2 minutes. Drain the potatoes and mash well, add the melted butter and chilli mixture and beat in. Keep warm.

3. Stir the snipped chives into the crème fraiche, season with a little salt and pepper. Set aside.

4. Lightly oil a heavy based frying pan or griddle pan and heat until very hot. Add the salmon fillets, skin-side down and cook for 2–3 minutes. Turn over and cook for a further 2–3 minutes until just cooked through.

5. Serve the salmon on top of the potato mash and serve with a dollop of crème fraiche on top. Garnish with fresh chives.

Preparation time: 20 min
Cooking time: 20 min
Serves 4

700g sweet potatoes
dash of lemon juice
50g butter
1 red chilli, deseeded and chopped
1 garlic clove, crushed
1 tbsp snipped chives
8 tbsp crème fraiche
salt and pepper to taste
olive oil to grease
4 salmon fillets
fresh chives, to serve

Fried redfish fillet with spinach and flaked almonds

Preparation time: 15 min
Cooking time: 20 min
Serves 4

450g spinach
3 tbsp butter
1 onion, finely chopped
zest and juice of 1 orange
4 tbsp crème fraiche
salt and pepper to taste
4 redfish fillets (also called 'red perch')
4 tbsp flour
2 tbsp lemon juice
2 tbsp flaked almonds, toasted, to serve

1. Wash the spinach and cook in a covered pan until just wilted. Drain well, chop and squeeze out any excess water.

2. Heat 2 tablespoons of the butter in a pan. Gently add the onion and cook until soft but not brown. Stir in the strained orange juice. Let the mixture begin to bubble. Add the crème fraiche. Season with salt and pepper. Stir in the spinach and set aside.

3. Wash the fish fillets and pat dry with kitchen paper. Season the flour with salt and pepper and place on a plate. Drizzle the lemon juice over the fish. Dredge in the seasoned flour.

4. Heat the remaining butter in a large frying pan. Fry the fish for 3–4 minutes on each side or until golden brown.

5. Garnish with the toasted almonds and orange zest. Serve with the spinach.

Clams with herb sauce

1. Heat the butter and oil in a large pan. Add the shallots and garlic and cook until soft but not brown.

2. Add the clams and the wine. Cover with a lid and cook for 3–4 minutes or until the clams have opened.

3. Stir in the remaining ingredients, discarding any clams that remain closed. Serve immediately.

Preparation time: 10 min
Cooking time: 10 min
Serves 4

2 tbsp butter
2 tbsp olive oil
2 shallots, finely chopped
3 garlic cloves, finely chopped
1.2kg clams, cleaned
125ml white wine
2 tbsp chopped parsley
2 tbsp chopped basil
2 tbsp chopped chervil

Baked cod fillet with mandarin oranges and mushrooms

1. Heat the oven to 180°C (375°F).

2. Rinse the cod in cold water and pat dry with kitchen paper. Season with salt and pepper and sprinkle with the lemon juice. Lay the pieces of fish in a baking dish brushed with oil.

3. Mix the cream with the curry powder. Drain the mandarin oranges, reserving 3 tablespoons of the juice. Stir this juice into the cream mixture.

4. Mix the spring onions, mushrooms and mandarin pieces into the cream and pour over the fish. Cover tightly with a kitchen foil and bake in the oven for about 15 minutes. Serve on plates, sprinkled with peppercorns.

Preparation time: 15 min
Cooking time: 15 min
Serves 4

4 pieces cod fillet
salt and pepper to taste
3 tbsp lemon juice
2 tbsp vegetable oil
250ml double cream
2 tsp curry powder
1 can mandarin oranges
4 spring onions, sliced
125g button mushrooms, sliced
1 tbsp red peppercorns, to serve

Trout wrapped in Parma ham

1. Wash the trout and pat dry with kitchen paper. Season the insides of the trout with salt and pepper. Rub the insides and the outside with the olive oil.

2. Heat the oven to 200°C (400°F). Stuff the cavities of the trout with the lemon slices, garlic and dried tomatoes.

3. Wrap each fish in 2 slices of Parma ham and place in an ovenproof dish. Bake in the oven for 20–25 minutes, basting from time to time, or until the fish is cooked through.

4. Garnish with the basil leaves.

Preparation time: 20 min
Cooking time: 25 min
Serves 4

4 trout, scaled and gutted
salt and pepper to taste
2 tbsp olive oil
2 lemons, sliced
2 garlic cloves, finely chopped
8 dried tomatoes in oil, roughly
   chopped
8 slices Parma ham
basil leaves, to serve

Paella

1. Heat the oil in a wide, shallow pan. Add the onion and garlic and gently cook until soft but not brown.

2. Add the pepper and chilli pepper. Stir for 2 minutes, then add the squid and the rice. Stir to coat the rice in the oil, then pour over the stock and add the saffron.

3. Bring to a simmer, season with salt and pepper and cook gently for 15 minutes. Add the chorizo, peas, mussels and clams. Cover with a lid and cook for 5–6 minutes or until the clams and mussels have opened and the rice is tender. Add a little water during the cooking if required.

4. Add the langoustines. Heat gently and drizzle over the lemon juice.

Preparation time: 15 min
Cooking time: 30 min
Serves 4

4 tbsp olive oil
1 onion, finely chopped
4 garlic cloves, finely chopped
1 red pepper, deseeded and finely chopped
2 red chilli peppers, deseeded and finely chopped
1 medium squid, cleaned and chopped
200g paella rice
500ml fish stock
2 pinches saffron threads
salt and pepper to taste
8 slices chorizo
150g frozen peas
450g mussels, cleaned
450g clams, cleaned
4 langoustines, cooked
juice of 1 lemon

King prawn and mango salad with coriander

1. Mix the prawns with 2 tablespoons of the oil, garlic and paprika. Set aside to marinate for 15 minutes.

2. Drop the spring onion into iced water so it begins to curl.

3. Heat the remaining oil in a frying pan. Add the prawns and cook for about 2 minutes, stirring frequently, or until cooked through.

4. Arrange the prawns, mango and spring onions on serving plates. Mix together the lime juice and maple syrup and drizzle over the salad.

5. Garnish with the chilli pepper and coriander.

Preparation time: 20 min
   plus 15 min marinating
Cooking time: 5 min
Serves 4

8 king prawns, peeled
5 tbsp olive oil
1 garlic clove, finely chopped
1 tsp paprika
1 spring onion, finely shredded
1 large ripe mango, peeled, stone removed and sliced
juice of 1 lime
1 tsp maple syrup
1 red chili pepper, deseeded and finely shredded, to serve
coriander leaves, to serve

Deep-fried catfish fillet with cucumber salsa

Preparation time: 20 min
Cooking time: 20 min
Serves 4

For the salsa:
1 cucumber, deseeded and
*   chopped*
1 garlic clove, crushed
4 tbsp olive oil
juice of 2 lemons
2 sprigs of dill, chopped
salt and pepper to taste

For the catfish:
450g catfish fillets, skinned and
*   chopped into chunks*
100g fine breadcrumbs
1 tbsp thyme leaves, chopped
4 tbsp flour
vegetable oil, for deep-frying
2 eggs, whisked

1. To make the salsa: mix together the cucumber, garlic, olive oil, lemon juice and chopped dill. Season with salt and pepper and set aside.

2. Wash the catfish chunks and pat dry with kitchen paper.

3. Mix the breadcrumbs with the chopped thyme and place on a plate.

4. Season the flour with salt and pepper and place on another plate.

5. Heat the oil in a deep pan until bubbles appear when a wooden spoon is dipped into the hot oil.

6. Dust the catfish pieces in the seasoned flour. Dip into the whisked egg, then into the breadcrumbs. Add to the oil and deep-fry the fish in batches until golden brown and crisp. Drain on kitchen paper and keep warm.

7. Serve with the salsa alongside.

Oysters au gratin with garlic and herbs

1. Heat the oven to 200°C (425°F).

2. Open and shuck the oysters, reserving the juice. Strain the oyster juice through a very fine sieve and set aside. Wash the deep oyster shells and set in a roasting pan with 1 oyster in each shell.

3. Heat the butter in a pan. Add the garlic and gently cook until soft but not brown. Stir in the breadcrumbs, herbs and lemon juice. Season with salt and pepper and spoon over the oysters.

4. Bake the oysters in the oven for about 5 minutes. Serve garnished with the sea salt and lemon wedges.

Preparation time: 20 min
Cooking time: 10 min
Serves 4

12 oysters
3 tbsp butter
4 garlic cloves, finely chopped
25g fresh breadcrumbs
2 tbsp chopped mixed herbs,
* parsley, tarragon, chervil*
juice of 1 lemon
salt flakes, to serve
lemon wedges to garnish

Pickled herring fillets on bean salad

1. For the fish, put the vinegar, water and sugar into a pan, bring to the boil and leave to cool.

2. Put the fish, vegetables and spices into a large preserving jar. Add the cold pickling liquor and seal the jar. Put in a cool place for at least 3 days.

3. For the bean salad, wash the frisee and rocket. Shake dry and tear into smaller pieces. Mix with the beans and dress with oil, vinegar, salt, pepper and lemon juice. Divide the salad between 4 plates.

4. Take the fish fillets out of the pickling liquor, drain and place on top of the salad. Serve immediately.

Preparation time: 15 min
  plus 72 h pickling
Cooking time: 5 min
Serves 4

For the herring:
250ml vinegar
200ml water
5 tbsp sugar
8 herring fillets, with skin
1 onion, roughly chopped
1 carrot, roughly chopped
1 tbsp coriander seeds
2 tsp peppercorns
1 star anise
1 tsp fennel seeds
2 bay leaves

For the bean salad:
A handful of frisee
A handful of rocket
225g cooked pinto beans, or borlotti
  beans
2 tbsp olive oil
1 tbsp balsamic vinegar
juice of 1 lemon

Tuna with tomato sauce

1. Heat the oven to 170°C (350°F). Season the tuna steaks with salt and pepper and place in an oiled baking dish.

2. Drop the tomatoes into boiling water for a few seconds. Refresh in cold water, then skin, quarter, deseed and chop the flesh finely.

3. Mix the olives and capers with the tomatoe. Add the Marsala and season to taste with salt and pepper.

4. Spread the tomato sauce on the tuna steaks, sprinkle with the breadcrumbs and drizzle with olive oil. Cover the dish with foil and bake the fish in the oven for about 30 minutes. Serve garnished with shredded basil.

Preparation time: 15 min
Cooking time: 30 min
Serves 4

4 fresh tuna steaks
salt and pepper to taste
700g tomatoes
100g black olives, pitted and finely
  chopped
2 tbsp capers, finely chopped
3 tbsp Marsala
4 tbsp breadcrumbs
4 tbsp olive oil
shredded basil, to garnish

Beetroot soup with matje herring and sour cream

Preparation time: 20 min
Cooking time: 30 min
Serves 4

300g beetroot, thinly sliced
1 1/5 litres beef stock
1 bay leaf
300g potatoes, peeled and thinly
   sliced
2 spring onions, sliced into rings
1 tbsp red wine vinegar
100ml sour cream
4 tbsp whipped cream
4 matje herring fillets, chopped
   into 2cm pieces
dill sprigs, to serve

1. Put the beetroot slices and stock in a pan with the bay leaf and bring to a boil. Cook for 10 minutes, then add the potato slices and a little salt. Cover and simmer for a further 10–15 minutes, until tender.

2. Add the spring onions and simmer for 2–3 minutes. Season to taste with salt, pepper and vinegar.

3. Mix the sour cream with the whipped cream.

4. Put the fish pieces into deep plates, ladle the beetroot soup over and top with a spoonful of cream. Serve garnished with dill sprigs.

Ciabatta sandwich with grilled tuna and peppers

1. Heat the grill or set the oven to the highest temperature.

2. Place the pepper slices under the grill or in the oven, slit-side down, until the skin darkens and blisters. Take out and cool, then remove skin.

3. Lay the tuna steaks on an oiled grill rack and grill for 2–3 minutes on each side. Season with salt and pepper. Drizzle a little lemon juice over the top and leave to cool slightly.

4. Put the garlic in a bowl with the mustard, vinegar, olive oil and mayonnaise, season with salt and pepper and mix to a make a dressing.

5. Halve the rolls and drizzle a little dressing over the top.

6. Arrange the peppers and radicchio leaves on the bottom halves of the rolls and place the tuna on top. Drizzle with dressing and cover with the top halves of the rolls.

Preparation time: 10 min
Cooking time: 15 min
Serves 2

1 yellow pepper, deseeded and
   chopped into 8 slices
2 fresh tuna steaks
salt and pepper to taste
juice of 1 lemon
1 small garlic clove, crushed
¼ tsp hot mustard
1 tbsp red wine vinegar
2 tbsp olive oil
4 tbsp mayonnaise
2 ciabatta rolls
4 radicchio leaves

Fish and tomato herby bake

1. Heat the oven to 200°C (400°F).

2. Place the potatoes in a baking dish. Add the oil and salt and mix gently.

3. Bake for 25–30 minutes until almost cooked. Remove from the oven and add the herbs and ham. Place the fish on top.

4. Mix the tomatoes, garlic, sugar and red wine. Season with salt and pepper. Pour evenly over the potatoes and fish.

5. Cover and bake for 15–20 minutes until the fish is cooked.

Preparation time: 15 min
Cooking time: 50 min
Serves 4

1kg new potatoes, halved
2 tbsp olive oil
2 sprigs marjoram
2 sprigs thyme
4 slices smoked ham
4 fish fillets, such as cod or perch
300g puréed tomatoes
2 garlic cloves, finely chopped
pinch sugar
50ml red wine
salt and pepper to taste

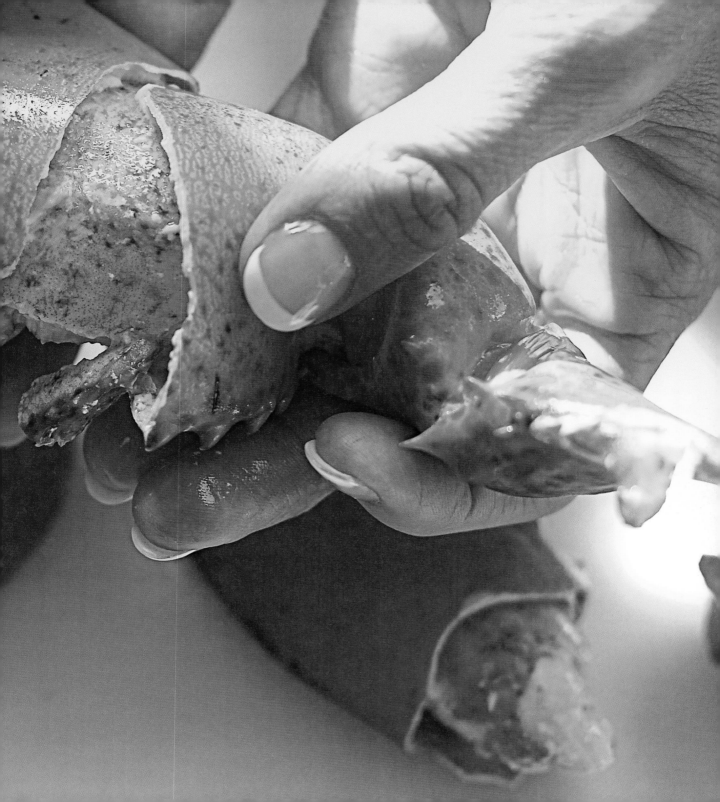

STEP 1 It is easiest to remove the meat from a lobster while it is still warm. To get to the meat, first twist off the claws and the head.

Preparing a lobster

Lobster looks and tastes impressive, but preparing it can seem daunting to the untrained eye. In fact, it's quite simple and takes less time than you would imagine.

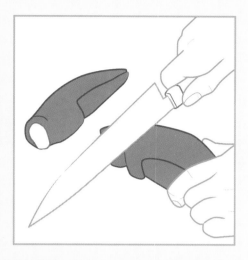

STEP 2 Take each claw and hold one end firmly. Using a heavy kitchen knife, crack open the shell, taking care not to cut into the flesh inside.

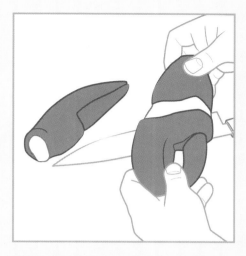

STEP 3 Remove the shell and pull out the flesh, using your fingers, in as large pieces as you can. Remove any tiny bits of shell with your fingers.

STEP 4 Using a heavy knife again, cut right through the shell of the tail of the lobster, splitting the piece in half.

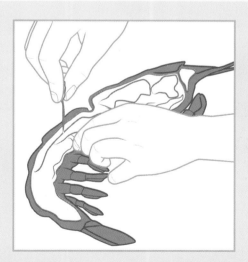

STEP 5 Using tweezers, carefully pull up and remove the dark intestinal tract that runs along the length of the tail.

Squid stuffed with olives

1. Heat the oven to 200°C (400°F). Butter an ovenproof baking dish.

2. Heat the oil in a frying pan. Add the onion, garlic and carrot and gently cook until softened. Add the tomatoes, cook for 5 minutes then add the pepper and courgette.

3. Cook for 2 minutes, then stir in the olives and chopped squid tentacles. Season to taste with salt and pepper and stuff the mixture into the squid bodies. Secure closed with cocktail sticks and place in the baking dish.

4. Spoon any remaining stuffing around the squids, pour over the wine and cover tightly with a tin foil.

5. Cook for 15–20 minutes or until the squid is cooked through. Serve garnished with black olives and thyme.

Preparation time: 15 min
Cooking time: 30 min
Serves 4

3 tbsp oil
1 onion, finely chopped
1 garlic clove, chopped
1 carrot, diced
2 large tomatoes, skinned,
   deseeded and chopped
1 red pepper, deseeded and diced
1 courgette, diced
100g green olives, pitted and sliced
4 medium squid, cleaned, tentacles
   chopped
salt and pepper to taste
125ml white wine
black olives and thyme sprigs,
   to serve

Fried trout with potato and pea rosti

1. Heat the oven to its lowest setting.

2. To make the rosti: peel the potatoes and grate them finely. Place the grated potato on a tea towel and wring it out well.

3. Mix in the thawed peas and the onion. Season with salt, pepper and nutmeg and knead in the flour and the egg.

4. Heat the oil and butter in a frying pan and fry the rosti, one at a time. Transfer to a plate and put them in the oven to keep warm.

5. While the rosti are frying, wash the herbs for the dip and shake them dry. Chop very finely.

6. Mix the crème fraiche with the milk. Add the herbs, the garlic salt and sugar.

7. Rinse the fish and pat dry. Slice into 5cm-long pieces, drizzle with lemon juice and season with salt and pepper.

8. Heat the oil and butter in a pan. Add each piece, skin-side down, and fry for about 1 minute. Turn the pieces over, and remove the pan from the heat.

9. Arrange the rosti on the heated plate and place the fish on top. Pour the dip into a small bowl and garnish with the dill and parsley.

Preparation time: 25 min
Cooking time: 20 min
Serves 4

For the rosti:
1kg floury potatoes
200g frozen peas, thawed
1 onion, finely diced
salt and pepper to taste
grated nutmeg
2 tbsp flour
1 egg
10 tbsp vegetable oil
2 tbsp butter

For the dip:
1 sprig dill
10 stalks chives
2 sprigs parsley
100g crème fraiche
2 tbsp milk
a pinch of garlic salt
a pinch of sugar

For the fish:
4 medium brook trout fillets,
  with skin
1 tbsp lemon juice
1 tbsp oil
1 tbsp butter

Dutch eel soup with capers and parsley

1. Heat the fish stock in a pan until simmering. Add the eel and cook for 10 minutes. Remove the eel with a slotted spoon and keep warm. Reserve the cooking liquor.

2. Melt the butter in a clean pan and add the flour. Cook, stirring all the time, for 2 minutes. Gradually add the vegetable stock and the eel cooking liquor. Simmer the liquid for 10 minutes.

3. Mix the cream with the egg yolks in a small bowl and whisk into the soup. Heat through very gently. Remove the pan from the heat and stir in the lemon juice and chopped parsley.

4. Season with salt and pepper. Ladle into warmed bowls and scatter over the capers. Add the cooked eel and garnish with the parsley leaves.

Preparation time: 15 min
Cooking time: 25 min
Serves 4

400ml fish stock
600g fresh eel, boned, skinned and sliced
2 tbsp butter
2 tbsp flour
400ml vegetable stock
4 tbsp double cream
2 egg yolks
juice of 1 lemon
2 tbsp chopped parsley
salt and pepper to taste
1 tbsp capers
parsley leaves, to serve

Fried catfish fillets with cress sauce

Preparation time: 10 min
Cooking time: 30 min
Serves 4

800g potatoes
5 tbsp butter
1 shallot, very finely chopped
125ml dry white wine
100ml double cream
salt and pepper to taste
8 catfish fillets (approximately
    125g each)
2 tbsp lemon juice
2–3 tbsp flour
3 tbsp cress
1 tbsp chopped parsley
lemon wedges, to serve

1. Place the potatoes in a pan of salted water. Heat until cooked. Drain well and set aside in a warm place until ready to serve.

2. Meanwhile, heat 2 tablespoons of the butter in a pan. Add the shallot and cook gently until soft but not brown.

3. Pour in the wine and simmer over a medium heat until reduced by about half. Stir in the cream, bring to a simmer and season to taste with salt and pepper.

4. Drizzle the fish fillets with the lemon juice. Sprinkle with salt and pepper and dredge with the flour. Shake off any excess flour.

5. Heat the remaining butter in a pan. Add the fillets and fry on each side over a medium heat for 2–3 minutes or until golden brown.

6. Place the fish onto warmed serving plates. Pour the sauce and scatter the cress over the fillets. Stir the parsley into the potatoes with a little butter and place on the plates. Garnish with the lemon wedges.

Steamed carp on a bed of courgettes and rocket

1. Sprinkle the lemon juice over the fish fillets and set aside.

2. Place the sesame seeds in a dry frying pan and toast until lightly browned. Set the seeds aside.

3. Heat 3 tablespoons of the oil alongwith the butter in the pan. Add the shallots and one clove of chopped garlic. Fry gently until soft but not brown.

4. Add the courgettes and 2 tablespoons of the wine and let the mixture begin to bubble. Add the rocket, put on a tightly fitting lid and cook gently for 5 minutes. Uncover and stir in the sesame seeds. Season with salt and pepper and set aside.

5. Meanwhile, place the remaining wine in the bottom of a steamer with a basket large enough to hold the carp fillets.

6. Lay the fillets in the basket and scatter the remaining garlic and oil over them. Season with the salt and pepper and steam for 6–8 minutes or until the fish is just cooked through.

7. Place the carp on a bed of the cooked courgettes and rocket. Garnish with the lemon wedges.

Preparation time: 15 min
Cooking time: 20 min
Serves 4

4 carp fillets, skinned
juice of 1 lemon
1 tbsp sesame seeds
4 tbsp olive oil
1 tbsp butter
2 shallots, finely chopped
2 garlic cloves, chopped
4 courgettes, cut into fine strips
250ml white wine
150g rocket, washed and roughly
  chopped
salt and pepper to taste
lemon wedges, to serve

Teriyaki salmon with pak choi

1. Wash and dry the salmon and place in a flat dish, skin-side up.

2. Mix together the teriyaki sauce, honey and lime juice and pour over the salmon. Cover and marinate for about 15 minutes.

3. Meanwhile, blanch the pak choi in boiling, salted water for about a minute. Drain well and pat dry.

4. Heat the sesame oil in a frying pan. Add the garlic and gently fry until soft. Pour over the pak choi and keep warm.

5. Heat the vegetable oil in a griddle pan. Add the salmon and fry skin-side down, sprinkling with about 4 tablespoons of the sauce. Cook for 2 minutes then turn over and continue cooking until the fish is just cooked through. Transfer to warmed serving plates and pour over the sauce from the pan.

6. Add a little more oil to the griddle pan and add the spring onions. Cook until soft. Arrange the spring onions on the fish and serve immediately with the pak choi alongside.

Preparation time: 15 min
  plus 15 min marinating
Cooking time: 15 min
Serves 4

4 salmon fillets, with skin
4 tbsp teriyaki sauce
2 tbsp honey
juice of 1 lime
450g pak choi, sliced vertically
3 tbsp sesame oil
2 garlic cloves, finely chopped
3 tbsp vegetable oil
4 spring onions, sliced vertically

Grilled gilthead bream with tomato and basil salsa

1. To make the salsa: drop the tomatoes into boiling water for 30 seconds. Peel, remove the seeds and chop the flesh.

2. Mix the chopped tomatoes with the remaining salsa ingredients, adding Tabasco to taste. Season with salt and pepper and set aside.

3. Heat the grill to its highest setting. Make diagonal slashes on both sides of the fish and rub the oil and lemon juice all over it. Tuck the rosemary and parsley into the cavity of the fish and secure the opening with a cocktail stick.

4. Grill the fish for 6–8 minutes on each side or until cooked through. Garnish with lemon slices and basil sprigs. Spoon the salsa over the fish.

Preparation time: 20 min
Cooking time: 15 min
Serves 4

For the salsa:
400g tomatoes
1 shallot, finely chopped
1 tbsp balsamic vinegar
1 tsp lemon juice
1 garlic clove, crushed
5 basil leaves, finely shredded
Tabasco sauce
salt and pepper to taste

For the fish:
1 large gilthead bream, scaled,
  gutted and trimmed
3 tbsp olive oil
2 tbsp lemon juice
1 sprig rosemary
2 sprigs parsley

To serve:
lemon slices
basil sprigs

Scallops with parsley and honey butter sauce

Preparation time: 20 min
Cooking time: 10 min
Serves 4

16 large scallops
3 tbsp butter
1 tbsp olive oil
2 garlic cloves, finely chopped
1 tbsp honey
juice of 1 lime
2 tbsp chopped parsley
parsley sprigs, to serve
salt and pepper to taste
lemon wedges, to serve

1. Wash the scallops and chop them in half horizontally.

2. Heat the butter and oil in a frying pan. Add the scallop pieces and fry for 1 minute on each side or until lightly browned. Remove from the pan and keep warm.

3. Add the garlic to the pan and cook gently until soft but not brown. Stir in the honey and lime juice. Allow the mixture to bubble. Add the parsley and season with salt and pepper. Remove the pan from the heat.

4. Place the scallops on warm plates. Pour the sauce over them and garnish with the parsley sprigs and lemon wedges.

Sole with lemon

1. Heat the oil in a large pan. Add the washed spinach and cook until wilted. Season with the salt and pepper and set aside.

2. Wash the sole and pat dry with kitchen paper. Season with salt and pepper. Heat the butter in a large frying pan. Add the sole fillets and gently cook for about 3 minutes on each side, basting with the butter as they cook.

3. Scatter the spring onions and parsley, and pour the lemon juice over the fillets. Let the juice begin to bubble. Serve the fish immediately with the spinach alongside and the pine nuts scattered over.

Preparation time: 15 min
Cooking time: 10 min
Serves 4

2 tbsp olive oil
4 large handfuls spinach, washed
salt and pepper to taste
4 sole fillets
2 tbsp butter
2 spring onions, sliced
2 tbsp chopped parsley
juice of 1 lemon
4 tbsp pine nuts, toasted, to serve

Sardines with fennel and lemon

1. Wash and trim the fennel bulbs and cut into eighths lengthwise. Cut the stalk out of each piece. Fill a wide pan to a depth of about 3cm with water and bring to a boil. Add the fennel bulbs and cover with a lid. Cook over a low heat for about 10 minutes, then drain thoroughly.

2. Wash the sardines and slit them open along their stomachs. Loosen the backbones with a knife or spoon handle and pull out. Cut off the heads, then wash, pat dry and season inside and out with salt and pepper.

3. Heat the oven to 200°C (400°F). Grease a baking dish and place the lemon slices, fennel bulbs and sardines in it. Add the garlic, wine and fennel seeds and drizzle with the olive oil.

4. Cover with a tin foil and bake the sardines in the oven for about 15 minutes. Garnish with the pine nuts and parsley.

Preparation time: 20 min
Cooking time: 25 min
Serves 4

2 bulbs fennel, sliced into wedges vertically
800g fresh sardines, cleaned
salt and pepper to taste
1 lemon, sliced
2 garlic cloves, chopped
125ml dry white wine
½ tsp fennel seeds
3 tbsp olive oil
1 tbsp pine nuts, toasted, to serve
parsley leaves, to serve

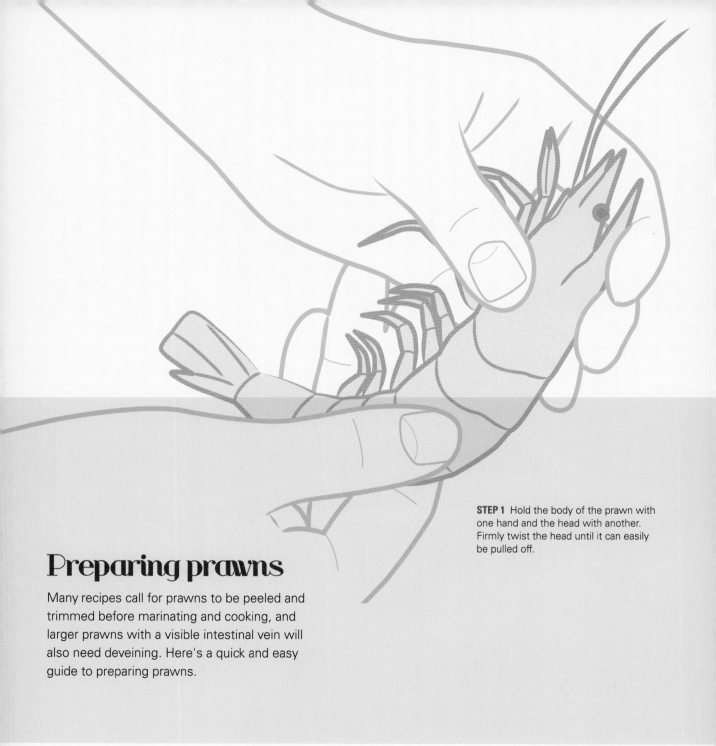

Preparing prawns

Many recipes call for prawns to be peeled and trimmed before marinating and cooking, and larger prawns with a visible intestinal vein will also need deveining. Here's a quick and easy guide to preparing prawns.

STEP 1 Hold the body of the prawn with one hand and the head with another. Firmly twist the head until it can easily be pulled off.

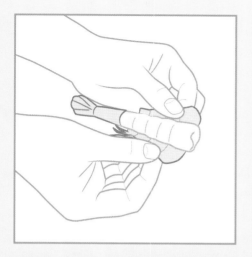

STEP 2 Split the soft shell along the underside of the prawn and gently pull it away from the flesh on the sides and back of the prawn.

STEP 3 The tail can be left on, or can be removed, if you prefer. Hold the body of the prawn with one hand and pull off the tail with the other.

STEP 4 Run the tip of a sharp filleting knife along the back of the prawn, cutting deep enough to expose the black intestinal vein.

STEP 5 Using the tip of the knife, carefully pull out the black vein and use the knife or your fingers to remove it from the prawn's flesh.

Red mullet in vine leaves

1. Rinse the mullet inside and out and pat dry with kitchen paper. Heat the oven to 200°C (400°F).

2. Mix the garlic with the herbes de Provence and the oil. Rub the fish inside and out with the mixture and set aside in a cool place for 30 minutes.

3. Meanwhile, wash and trim the fennel and set the leaves to one side. Chop the bulb into quarters, remove the stalk and cut the fennel into thin strips using a mandolin slicer. Chop the leaves finely.

4. Mix the fennel strips, leaves, tomatoes and chopped parsley together. Season with the salt and pepper and place in the cavities of the fish with the lemon slices.

5. Rinse the vine leaves and pat dry, then spread them out close to each other. Rub salt on the fish and lay each one on vine leaves. Wrap tightly so the bodies are covered but the heads and tails are still visible. Tie the leaves in place with a kitchen string.

6. Lay the fish in a greased ovenproof dish. Drizzle a little olive oil over them and cover with a foil. Bake for 20–25 minutes. Remove the string and garnish with the fresh herbs and lemon wedges.

Preparation time: 15 min
  plus 30 min resting
Cooking time: 25 min
Serves 4

4 medium red mullet, scaled and
  gutted
2 garlic cloves, finely chopped
1 tsp herbes de Provence
3 tbsp olive oil
1 bulb fennel bulb
100g cherry tomatoes, quartered
4 tbsp chopped parsley
salt and pepper to taste
4 slices lemon
20 pickled vine leaves
mixed fresh herbs, to garnish
lemon wedges, to garnish

Mackerel on tomatoes with basil

1. Heat 2 tablespoons of the oil in a large frying pan and gently cook the garlic until it just starts to brown.

2. Add the tomatoes and basil, season with salt and pepper and cook for 2 minutes. Stir in about 1 teaspoon of the lemon juice then remove from the pan and keep warm.

3. Wash the mackerel and pat dry with kitchen paper. Rub the remaining lemon juice over the fish, inside and out, and season with salt and pepper.

4. Wipe the pan clean with kitchen paper and add the remaining oil. Heat until the oil begins to smoke. Add the fish and fry for about 10 minutes, turning carefully from time to time, or until the fish is nicely browned and cooked through.

5. Serve with the tomato preparation.

Preparation time: 15 min
Cooking time: 15 min
Serves 4

4 tbsp olive oil
2 garlic cloves, sliced
4 large tomatoes, deseeded and
   flesh chopped
2 sprigs basil, leaves only
salt and pepper to taste
juice of 1 lemon
4 mackerel, heads removed, scaled
   and gutted

Texan red snapper fillet with vegetables cooked in foil

1. Heat the oven to 180°C (375°F).

2. Heat the oil in a pan and add the shallot, garlic and chilli pepper. Gently cook until soft but not brown.

3. Add the tinned tomatoes, tomato purée and sugar. Simmer gently, stirring from time to time, until the sauce is thick. Season with salt and pepper and set aside.

4. Sprinkle the fish fillets with the lemon juice and season with salt and pepper. Lay each fillet on a large piece of tin foil. Spoon the sauce and scatter the celery and corn cobs over the fillets. Bring the edges of the foil together to make a parcel and place in a roasting pan.

5. Bake in the oven for 25–30 minutes or until the fish is cooked through. Serve immediately.

Preparation time: 15 min
Cooking time: 35 min
Serves 4

3 tbsp oil
1 shallot, finely chopped
2 garlic cloves, chopped
1 red chilli pepper, deseeded and
  finely chopped
200g tinned tomatoes, chopped
2 tbsp tomato purée
1 tsp sugar
salt and pepper to taste
4 red snapper fillets
juice of 1 lemon
2 sticks celery, chopped
16 baby corn cobs

Fish fillet with potato and mustard crust, and beetroot

Preparation time: 15 min
Cooking time: 30 min
Serves 2

2 large cod fillets, or any other
   white fish
2 small potatoes, peeled and
   grated
2 tbsp butter
2 spring onions, finely sliced
1 tbsp Dijon mustard
1 tsp creamed horseradish
salt and pepper to taste
125 ml white wine

In addition:
2 beetroots, vacuum-packed,
   cooked
1 onion, sliced
2 tbsp vinegar
1 sprig dill

1. Heat the oven to 170°C (350°F).

2. Wash the fish and pat dry with kitchen paper. Rinse the grated potato in a sieve and squeeze out any excess moisture in a clean tea towel.

3. Melt the butter in a small pan. Add the potato and spring onions and gently cook until soft. Stir in the mustard and horseradish.

4. Season the fish with salt and pepper and place in a buttered ovenproof dish. Spread the potato mixture on top of the fish, pour the wine around it and cover with tin foil. Bake in the oven for 20–30 minutes or until the fish is cooked through.

5. For the beetroot salad, cut the beetroot into chunks and mix with the onion and vinegar. Season with salt and pepper.

6. Place the fish on warmed plates. Add the beetroot salad next to it and garnish with the dill.

Scallops with salsa verde and pan-fried cauliflower

1. To make the salsa verde: place the parsley, basil, mint, anchovies, garlic and capers in a food processor. Add the lemon juice and gradually pour in the olive oil whilst the motor is running. Season to taste with salt and ground black pepper.

2. Cook the cauliflower in boiling, salted water for 5–7 minutes or until just tender. Drain well and set aside.

3. Heat 2 tablespoons of the butter in a skillet. Add the breadcrumbs and fry until lightly browned. Add the cauliflower florets and toss them in the buttered breadcrumbs for 2 minutes.

4. Season the scallops with salt and pepper. Heat the remaining butter in a clean pan and add the scallops. Fry for 2 minutes on each side.

5. Serve with the salsa verde and cauliflower.

Preparation time: 25 min
Cooking time: 15 min
Serves 4

25g parsley, chopped
25g basil, chopped
25g mint, chopped
4 anchovy fillets, chopped
1 garlic clove, crushed
2 tbsp capers
2 tbsp lemon juice
8 tbsp olive oil
1 cauliflower, broken into florets
4 tbsp butter
2 tbsp breadcrumbs
12 shelled scallops

Crayfish risotto

1. Place the crayfish in a large pot of water with the bay leaves, peppercorns, thyme and onion. Bring to a boil and simmer for 10 minutes.

2. Strain the crayfish, reserving the liquid, and peel the tails. Reserve some of the heads and tails for the garnish. Set the tail meat aside.

3. Heat the butter in a wide pan and gently cook the onion and garlic until soft but not brown. Add the carrot and tomatoes and cook for 1 minute.

4. Stir in the rice and pour over the wine. Let the wine evaporate then add one ladle of the crayfish liquid. Stir until the liquid has been absorbed by the rice then add another ladle of the liquid. Continue cooking like this, stirring all the time, until the rice is tender. You may need to add a little water.

5. Stir in the peas, lemon juice and crayfish tails. Season with salt and pepper. Spoon onto warmed serving dishes. Scatter the parsley over the mixture. Garnish with the sage leaves and the reserved crayfish shells.

Preparation time: 10 min
Cooking time: 30 min
Serves 2

1kg fresh crayfish
2 bay leaves
4 peppercorns
1 sprig thyme
1 white onion, roughly chopped
3 tbsp butter
1 red onion, finely chopped
2 garlic cloves, chopped
1 carrot, finely chopped
4 tomatoes, deseeded and finely
  chopped
200g risotto rice
125ml white wine
150g frozen peas
juice of 1 lemon
salt and pepper to taste
2 tbsp chopped parsley
sage leaves, to serve

Crabmeat with green asparagus

1. Steam the asparagus until just tender.

2. Meanwhile, mix the crabmeat with the lemon juice and season with salt and pepper.

3. Arrange the shredded lettuce in tightly packed circles on the middle of 4 serving plates.

4. Shape the crabmeat into 4 patties and lay them on top of the lettuce.

5. Mix the olive oil with the lemon zest and season with salt and pepper. Arrange the marjoram around the crab and drizzle with the olive oil dressing.

6. Coat the steamed asparagus with the melted butter and arrange on top of the crab. Serve immediately.

Preparation time: 20 min
Cooking time: 10 min
Serves 4

12 asparagus spears
450g white crabmeat
juice and zest of 1 lemon
salt and pepper to taste
2 handfuls mixed salad leaves,
*   finely shredded*
3 tbsp olive oil
1 tbsp marjoram leaves
1 tbsp butter, melted

Cod fillets au gratin with mashed potatoes and leeks

Preparation time: 25 min
Cooking time: 30 min
Serves 4

500g floury potatoes, peeled and washed
3 tbsp olive oil
1 red onion, finely chopped
2 tomatoes, deseeded and chopped
50g fresh breadcrumbs
3 tbsp grated Parmesan cheese
zest and juice of 1 lemon
2 tbsp chopped basil leaves
salt and pepper to taste
4 tbsp butter
2 leeks, finely sliced
125ml milk
1 tbsp vegetable oil
4 cod fillets
basil leaves, to serve

1. Place the peeled potatoes in a pan of salted water. Bring to a boil and cook until tender.

2. Meanwhile, heat the olive oil in a pan and add the onions. Cook until soft but not brown. Add the tomatoes and cook for a further 5 minutes.

3. Mix in the breadcrumbs, Parmesan, lemon zest and basil leaves. Season with salt and pepper and set aside.

4. Heat the butter in a clean pan and add the leeks. Cook until soft.

5. Drain the potatoes, return to the pan and add the milk. Mash until smooth and season with salt and pepper and stir in the leeks.

6. Heat the grill to its highest setting.

7. Season the cod fillets with the lemon juice, salt and pepper. Heat the vegetable oil in a pan and gently fry the fillets for 2–3 minutes on each side.

8. Cover the cod with the tomato mixture and grill for about 2 minutes.

9. Place the cod on a bed of mash with the basil leaves scattered over it.

Stuffed squid with garlic

1. Separate the tentacles from the squid bodies and roughly chop the tentacles.

2. Heat the oil in a wide pan. Add the onion and garlic, and cook gently until soft but not browned. Add the chilli pepper and carrot and continue cooking very gently for 5 minutes.

3. Stir in the breadcrumbs, season with salt and pepper, and remove from the heat. Stuff a few pieces of chopped tentacle into the body of each squid then spoon in some of the breadcrumb stuffing. Close the bodies with a cocktail stick.

4. Wipe the pan clean and add a little more oil. Heat gently then add the stuffed squids. Add the rosemary and thyme. Pour the wine over the mixture and cook gently, covered with a lid, for about 15 minutes, shaking the pan from time to time.

5. Remove the lid, turn up the heat and let the wine evaporate. Serve immediately.

Preparation time: 15 min
Cooking time: 35 min
Serves 4

16 baby squid, cleaned
3 tbsp olive oil
1 onion, finely chopped
4 garlic cloves, finely chopped
1 red chilli pepper, deseeded and
  finely chopped
1 small carrot, peeled and finely
  chopped
50g fresh breadcrumbs
salt and pepper to taste
1 sprig rosemary
1 sprig thyme
125ml white wine

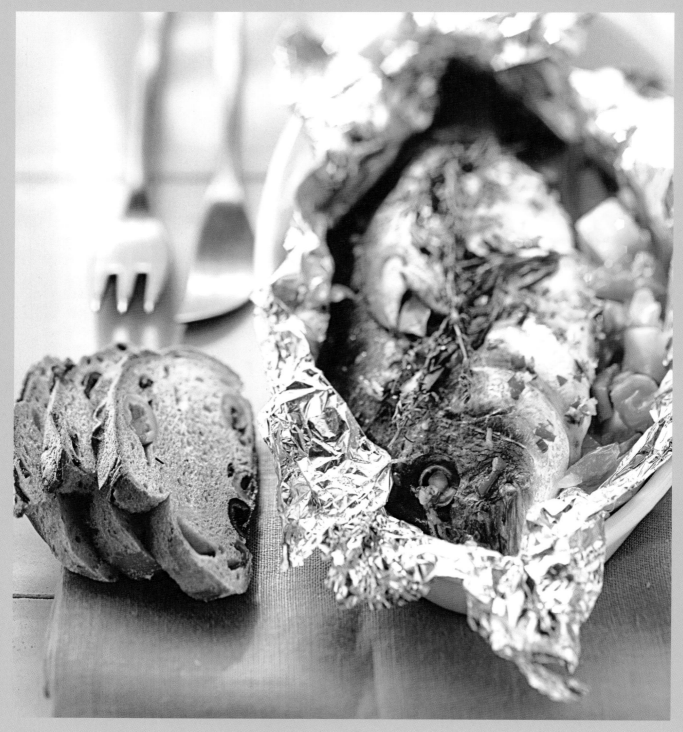

Braised gilthead sea bream in foil

1. Heat the oven to 200°C (400°F).

2. Wash the fish and pat dry. Rub the insides with the lemon juice and season with salt and pepper.

3. Heat 4 tablespoons of the oil in a pan. Add the onion and cook gently until soft but not brown. Add the garlic, chilli and potato and continue cooking for 2 minutes. Remove the pan from the heat and set aside.

4. Brush 2 double-layered sheets of tin foil with a little oil and place a fish in the middle of each one. Place a little of the onion mixture into the cavities and spread the remaining on top. Draw up the edges of the foil and scatter in the bell pepper and tomatoes. Lay the herbs on top of the fish, pour over the wine and season with salt and pepper.

5. Seal the edges of the foil to make parcels and place them in a large roasting pan. Roast in the oven for 25–30 minutes or until the fish is cooked through.

Preparation time: 15 min
Cooking time: 35 min
Serves 4

2 gilthead sea bream, scaled and
  gutted
juice of 1 lemon
salt and pepper to taste
6 tbsp olive oil
1 onion, finely chopped
3 garlic cloves, chopped
2 red chillies, deseeded and finely
  chopped
1 medium potato, peeled and diced
2 tbsp chopped parsley
1 green pepper, deseeded and
  chopped
2 tomatoes, deseeded and chopped
2 bay leaves
4 sprigs thyme
4 sprigs rosemary
125ml white wine

Monkfish fricassee

1. Wash the monkfish and pat dry with kitchen paper.

2. Heat the butter in a wide pan and add the lemon slices, peppercorns, wine and fish stock. Place the fish steaks in the pan. Bring to a simmer and cook gently for 8–10 minutes or until the fish is just cooked through.

3. Remove the fish with a slotted spoon and set aside in a warm place. Strain the cooking liquid through a fine sieve and set aside.

4. For the vegetables, wipe the pan clean and heat the butter in it. Add the carrots, leeks and salsify. Cook gently for 3 minutes, stirring to coat the vegetables in the butter. Add the morels and about 250ml of the fish cooking liquid.

5. Bring to a simmer and cook gently for 6–8 minutes or until the vegetables are tender. Baste the vegetables with the liquid during cooking.

6. Remove the vegetables with a slotted spoon and place onto warm serving dishes with the fish. Add the cream to the pan and bring to a simmer. Season with salt and pepper.

Preparation time: 15 min
Cooking time: 30 min
Serves 4

4 monkfish steaks
1 tbsp butter
4 slices lemon
6 peppercorns
125ml dry white wine
125ml fish stock

For the vegetables:
50g butter
4 carrots, chopped into sticks
2 leeks, sliced
2 sticks salsify, peeled and chopped
   into batons
4 morel mushrooms, brushed clean
175ml double cream
salt and pepper to taste

For the garnish:
parsley sprigs

Lobster thermidor

1. Slice the lobsters in half lengthways. Break off the claws and separate the meat from the claws and tail.

2. Chop the meat and return it to the body of the lobster.

3. Heat the butter in a small pan. Add the shallot and cook gently until soft but not brown. Add the stock and wine. Bring to a simmer, then reduce by about a half.

4. Add the cream and mustard. Simmer until thick, then add the lemon juice and season with salt and pepper.

5. Heat the grill to its highest setting. Pour the sauce over the lobsters and grill until brown and bubbling. Serve immediately.

Preparation time: 15 min
Cooking time: 30 min
Serves 2

2 small lobsters, cooked
3 tbsp butter
1 shallot, finely chopped
250ml fish stock
3 tbsp white wine
125ml double cream
1 tsp mustard
1 tbsp lemon juice
salt and pepper to taste

Turbot fillet with olive dressing on julienne vegetables

1. Heat the butter in a large wide pan. Add the vegetables. Cook for 2 minutes and add the stock. Bring to a simmer and lay the fish on top. Cover and cook for about 6 minutes or until the fish is just cooked through.

2. Meanwhile, mix together the olives, olive oil and lemon juice. Stir in the thyme leaves and season with salt and pepper. Set aside.

3. Place the fish on a bed of vegetables and spoon the olive dressing on top.

Preparation time: 20 min
Cooking time: 8 min
Serves 4

2 tbsp butter
1 courgette, finely julienned
1 red pepper, deseeded and finely
  julienned
2 carrots, peeled and finely julienned
125ml vegetable stock
4 turbot fillets
50g green olives, finely chopped
50g black olives, finely chopped
3 tbsp olive oil
juice of 1 lemon
2 tsp chopped thyme leaves
salt and pepper to taste

Octopus ragout with chestnuts and onions

Preparation time: 20 min
Cooking time: 2 h 55 min
Serves 4

1 large octopus, cleaned
250ml white wine
1 bay leaf
1 sprig thyme
6 peppercorns
3 tbsp olive oil
1 onion, finely chopped
2 garlic cloves, finely chopped
1 tsp paprika
2 red chilli peppers, deseeded and
  finely chopped
1 tbsp tomato purée
salt and pepper to taste
2 German sausages, thickly sliced
400g chestnuts, cooked and peeled
chopped parsley, to serve

1. Blanch the octopus in a large pan of salted water for 2 minutes. Drain, slice and discard the head.

2. Heat the oven to 180°C (350°F).

3. Place the octopus tentacles in a large ovenproof pot with the wine, bay leaf, thyme and peppercorns. Cover the pot with a tightly fitting lid and cook for 2 hours, basting from time to time. Add a little water if it looks dry.

4. Heat the oil in a large saucepan. Add the onion and gently cook until soft but not brown. Add the garlic and paprika, and cook for 1 minute. Add the chilli pepper and tomato purée.

5. Add the sausage and brown well. Strain the octopus, reserving the liquid, and discard the herbs and peppercorns.

6. Chop the tentacles into large pieces and add to the pan with the sausage mixture. Add the reserved liquid. Season with salt and pepper. Add the chestnuts and about 1 cup of water.

7. Cover the pan and cook gently for about 40 minutes or until the octopus is tender. Garnish with the chopped parsley.

Prawn and cucumber terrine with sour cream

1. Sprinkle the cucumber with the salt and leave it to drain in a sieve.

2. Mix the sour cream, yoghurt, lemon juice and horseradish and season to taste with pepper, cayenne pepper and salt.

3. Put the gelatine into a pan, dripping wet, and dissolve over a low heat. Stir into the cream mixture and divide the mixture between 2 bowls.

4. Set aside some of the lemon zest to garnish. Mix the chopped dill and the squeezed-out cucumber into one bowl, and mix the prawns and the remaining lemon zest into the other half.

5. Line a 1 litre terrine dish with plastic wrap. Spread the dill mixture smoothly in the bottom and put into the freezer for 10 minutes.

6. Add the shrimp mixture, cover and refrigerate to set for at least 6 hours.

7. To serve, turn the terrine out onto a platter and garnish with the watercress, dill sprigs, lemon zest, lemon slices and dill flowers.

Preparation time: 35 min
plus 6 h chilling
Cooking time: 5 min
Serves 4

1 large cucumber, peeled, deseeded
and finely chopped
1 tsp salt
500ml sour cream
250ml yoghurt
juice of 1 lemon
2 tsp horseradish cream
cayenne pepper
7 sheets white gelatine, soaked in
cold water
2 sprigs dill, chopped
250g cooked peeled prawns, roughly
chopped
zest of 1 lemon
½ bunch watercress, to serve
dill sprigs and flowers, to serve
lemon slices, to serve

Trout provençale with tomato ragout, capers and herbs

1. Heat the oven to 180°C (375°F).

2. Mix the parsley, mustard, breadcrumbs and melted butter. Season with salt and pepper and set aside.

3. Drop the tomatoes into boiling water for 30 seconds, then refresh in cold water. Skin and roughly chop the flesh.

4. Heat the oil in a flameproof roasting pan and briefly sweat the tomatoes with the garlic, rosemary, capers and bay leaves. Season with salt and pepper.

5. Lay the trout fillets side by side on top of the tomatoes, skin-side up. Spread the breadcrumb mixture along the fish fillets. Bake in the oven for 15–20 minutes or until the fish is cooked through.

6. Spoon the tomato ragout onto warmed plates and place the trout fillets on top.

Preparation time: 15 min
Cooking time: 25 min
Serves 4

2 tbsp chopped parsley
2 tbsp grain mustard
100g fresh breadcrumbs
4 tbsp butter, melted
salt and pepper to taste
6 large tomatoes
4 tbsp olive oil
2 garlic cloves, chopped
4 sprigs rosemary
2 tbsp capers
8 bay leaves
4 whole trout fillets

120

Turbot with beetroot salsa and couscous

1. Place the couscous into a bowl, stir in the stock, cover and leave to stand for 10 minutes.

2. Meanwhile, make the beetroot salsa, place all the ingredients in a bowl and mix well. Season to taste.

3. Mix the flour with a little salt and pepper and dust the turbot fillets with the flour. Heat a little oil in a heavy based frying pan and add the fish. Fry for 3–4 minutes each side until tender.

4. Whilst the fish is cooking, uncover the couscous and fluff up with a fork. Add the herbs, spring onions and tomatoes and toss well. Season to taste.

5. Serve the turbot with the couscous and beetroot salsa.

Preparation time: 25 min
Cooking time: 10 min
Serves 4

1 tbsp plain flour
salt and pepper to taste
4 turbot fillets
oil, for frying

For the couscous:
100g couscous
200ml hot vegetable stock
4 tbsp chopped fresh parsley
2 tbsp chopped fresh mint
4 spring onions, trimmed and sliced
4 SunBlush tomatoes, sliced

For the beetroot salsa:
4 cooked beetroots, diced
1 small red onion, finely chopped
1 red chilli, seeded and chopped
2 tbsp chopped fresh mint
2 tbsp chopped fresh parsley
2 tbsp lemon juice
5 tbsp olive oil

Fish cakes with speedy hollandaise

Preparation time: 25 min
   plus 30 min chilling
Cooking time: 25 min
Serves 4

For the fish cakes:
600g pollack or cod fillet, skinned
1 tsp peppercorns
juice 1 lemon
1 tbsp capers, roughly chopped
2 tbsp fresh dill, chopped
2 tbsp mayonnaise
400g potatoes, peeled, boiled and
   mashed
3 tbsp plain flour
sunflower oil, for frying

For the hollandaise:
175g butter
2 egg yolks
1 tbsp white wine vinegar
1 tbsp lemon juice
salt and pepper to taste

To garnish:
dill sprigs

1. Place the fish into a wide pan. Cover with cold salted water and the peppercorns. Bring to a boil and simmer gently for 5–7 minutes, or until the fish flakes easily.

2. Use a slotted spoon to lift the fish from the liquid and place into a bowl.

3. Add the lemon juice, capers, dill, mayonnaise and mashed potato. Season with salt and ground black pepper and mix well.

4. Lightly flour a work surface and knead the mix to form 8 fishcakes. Chill for 30 minutes.

5. Meanwhile, make the hollandaise sauce. Melt the butter in a small pan over a medium heat, making sure it does not burn. Turn off the heat and allow the milky residue to settle to the bottom of the pan.

6. Place the egg yolks in a food processor. Add the vinegar and lemon juice. Blend for 15 seconds.

7. With the processor running slowly, gradually drip the melted butter through the feeder tube in the lid, leaving the milky residue behind. Season with salt and pepper and set aside in a warm place.

8. Heat the sunflower oil in a large skillet. Add the fish cakes and fry for 3–4 minutes on each side, turning once, until golden. Garnish with fresh dill and warm hollandaise sauce.

Prawn strudel with tomato salad and basil aioli

1. Heat the oven to 180°C (375°F).

2. Roughly chop the zander or perch and place in a food processor. Add the chilli pepper, cream, cayenne and lemon juice. Blend the mixture until smooth. Stir in the prawns and season with salt and pepper.

3. Place one sheet of strudel pastry on a greased cookie sheet. Brush the pastry with melted butter. Place the second sheet of pastry on top and lay the fish mixture along the centre lengthways.

4. Roll the pastry up to form a long parcel and brush with the remaining butter. Bake in the oven for 25–30 minutes or until golden brown.

5. For the basil aioli: tear the leaves from the basil sprigs and place in a food processor with the egg yolk, mustard and garlic. Blend together then add the oil in a slow stream while the motor is still running. Stir in the lemon juice, season with salt and pepper and set aside.

6. For the tomato salad: mix together the honey, oil and vinegar to make a dressing. Mix the remaining ingredients together, stir in the dressing and season with sea salt.

7. Place the tomato salad on serving plates, spoon over the basil aioli and top with a slice of the strudel. Serve garnished with the parsley sprigs.

Preparation time: 30 min
Cooking time: 30 min
Serves 4

For the strudel:
250g zander or perch fillets, cleaned and skinned
1 red chilli pepper, deseeded and chopped
250ml double cream
cayenne pepper
juice of ½ lemon
350g prawns, peeled and chopped
salt and pepper to taste
2 sheets strudel pastry
3 tbsp butter, melted

For the basil aioli:
1 bunch basil
1 egg yolk
1 tsp strong mustard
1 garlic clove
175ml olive oil
1 tsp lemon juice

For the tomato salad:
1 tsp honey
3 tbsp olive oil
1 tbsp white wine vinegar
12 red cherry tomatoes, halved
12 yellow cherry tomatoes, halved
2 rashers bacon, chopped and fried
2 shallots, finely chopped
2 tbsp parsley, chopped, plus sprigs to serve

Mackerel nicoise salad

1. Boil the potatoes in salted water until just tender. Peel, chop into quarters and set aside.

2. Meanwhile, boil the eggs for 7 minutes. Run under cold water and peel off the shells. Chop into quarters and set aside.

3. Blanch the beans in boiling water for 3 minutes. Drain, refresh under cold running water and set aside.

4. Heat the grill to its highest setting. Make diagonal slashes in the skin of the fish and rub a little oil over it. Grill the fish skin-side up for about 4 minutes or until cooked through.

5. Meanwhile, mix the remaining oil with the lemon juice and season with salt and pepper to make a dressing.

6. Place the potatoes, beans, lettuce, tomatoes, anchovies, olives and capers in a large bowl and gently mix in the dressing. Arrange onto serving plates. Add the eggs and top with the grilled fish.

Preparation time: 15 min
Cooking time: 30 min
Serves 4

8 new potatoes
2 eggs
250g green beans
4 mackerel fillets
4 tbsp olive oil
juice of 1 lemon
salt and pepper to taste
8 batavia lettuce leaves,
*   roughly torn*
8 cherry tomatoes, halved
8 tinned anchovy fillets
50g black olives
1 tbsp capers, drained and
*   rinsed*

STEP 1 Scrub the shells of the oysters thoroughly under cold running water using a scrubbing brush. Only use closed oysters; if the shells are even a fraction open, discard them.

Shucking an oyster

Oysters, unlike many shellfish, are served raw. However, although they do not need cooking, they do need 'shucking' or opening before serving.

STEP 2 Wrap a towel around one hand and hold the oyster in it, with the flat side of the shell uppermost. Push the point of an oyster knife into the hinge.

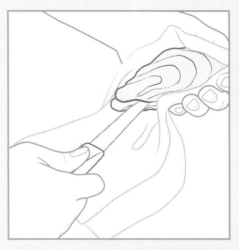

STEP 3 With the point of the knife inserted, work the blade between the top and bottom shells with a little force until the hinge breaks.

STEP 4 Twist the point of the knife upwards to lever up the top half of the shell. Cut through the ligament joining the shells and remove the top shell.

STEP 5 Loosen the oyster in the serving shell by gently sliding the tip of the knife underneath it, taking care not to slice through the oyster meat.

Cod with hazelnut crust

1. Wash the cod and pat dry with kitchen paper. Sprinkle with a little of the lemon juice and place in a steamer.

2. Pour about a cup of water into the bottom of the steamer and add the wine. Steam the fish for about 10 minutes or until nearly cooked through.

3. Meanwhile, heat the olive oil in a frying pan. Add the garlic and gently fry until soft but not brown. Add the breadcrumbs and hazelnuts and cook until lightly browned. Stir in the lemon zest and the remaining juice and season with salt and pepper.

4. Place the fish on warmed serving plates. Top with the crust and serve garnished with the chopped chives.

Preparation time: 15 min
Cooking time: 15 min
Serves 4

4 cod fillets
juice and zest of 1 lemon
125ml white wine
3 tbsp olive oil
2 garlic cloves, finely chopped
75g fresh breadcrumbs
175g chopped hazelnuts
salt and pepper to taste
chopped chives, to serve

Gourmet fish fingers with remoulade sauce

1. For the remoulade, mix together the sour cream, yoghurt, mayonnaise, shallots and mustard. Reserve a little of the dill pickles, chopped eggs and chives for the garnish. Stir the remainder into the sour cream mixture. Add the sugar, season with salt and pepper and set aside.

2. For the fish fingers, wash the fish chunks and pat dry on kitchen paper. Mix in the lemon juice, season with salt and pepper and set aside.

3. Heat the vegetable oil in a deep pan for deep-frying. When bubbles appear on dipping a wooden spoon into the hot oil, it is ready.

4. Dredge the fish pieces in the flour. Dip into the whisked eggs and then into the breadcrumbs, ensuring they are completely coated.

5. Fry the fish pieces in batches in the oil for 4–6 minutes or until they are golden brown and cooked through. Drain on kitchen paper and keep warm while you cook the remaining fish.

6. Place the remoulade in a small bowl and garnish with the reserved dill pickles, egg and chives. Serve the fish fingers garnished with lettuce and the remoulade sauce alongside.

Preparation time: 20 min
Cooking time: 10 min
Serves 4

For the remoulade sauce:
175ml sour cream
175ml yoghurt
3 tbsp mayonnaise
2 shallots, finely chopped
1 tsp mustard
100g dill pickles, chopped
2 eggs, hard-boiled and chopped
3 tbsp chopped chives
pinch sugar
salt and pepper to taste

For the fish fingers:
800g white fish fillets, cut into
  chunks
1 tbsp lemon juice
vegetable oil, for deep-frying
100g flour
2 eggs, whisked
200g breadcrumbs
lettuce, to serve

Barramundi fillet en papillote

1. Wash the tomatoes and drop them into boiling water for a few seconds. Skin, remove the seeds and chop the flesh.

2. Place the tomatoes, garlic, almonds, 1 tablespoon of parsley, the basil and oil in a blender or food processor. Pulse quickly to make a coarse paste.

3. Wash the fish and pat dry with kitchen paper. Spread the puréed tomato mixture on both sides of the fish and set aside to marinade for 1 hour.

4. Heat the oven to 200°C (400°F). Divide parchment paper into 4 pieces big enough to hold the fish and lay a slice of fish on each piece. Spoon over the tomato mixture, remaining parsley and lime juice. Season with salt and pepper. Fold into a parcel and scrunch the edges to seal.

5. Place on the parcels in a roasting pan and cook for 15–20 minutes. Before serving, open each parcel and sprinkle the fish with the spring onions. Serve immediately, garnished with lime wedges and coriander leaves.

Preparation time: 15 min
 plus 1 h marinating
Cooking time: 20 min
Serves 4

6 ripe tomatoes
2 garlic cloves, roughly chopped
1 tbsp ground, blanched almonds
2 tbsp chopped parsley
1 tbsp chopped basil
4 tbsp olive oil
4 pieces barramundi fillet
juice of 2 limes
4 spring onions, cut into thin rings
lime wedges, to serve
coriander leaves, to serve
salt and pepper to taste

Baked sea trout with tomato salad

Preparation time: 10 min
Cooking time: 35 min
Serves 4

*2 large sea trout fillets, about 600g
  each
3 tbsp butter
2 tbsp chopped parsley
juice and zest of 1 lemon
125ml white wine
salt and pepper to taste*

*For the tomato salad:
4 large tomatoes, chopped
1 shallot, finely chopped
1 garlic clove, finely chopped
1 tbsp chopped mint
4 tbsp olive oil
1 tbsp balsamic vinegar*

1. Heat the oven to 200°C (400°F).

2. Place one fillet of fish skin-side down in an ovenproof dish. Dot the butter over the flesh. Sprinkle with the parsley, lemon juice and zest and place the other fillet, skin-side up, on top.

3. Pour over the wine, season with salt and pepper and cover with a tin foil. Bake in the oven for about 35 minutes or until the fish is cooked through. Baste the fish twice during the cooking.

4. For the salad: mix all the ingredients together, season with salt and pepper and set aside.

5. Serve the fish with the salad.

Breaded perch with mushrooms

1. Heat the oven to 200°C (400°F).

2. Wash the perch and pat dry. Rub the inside of the fish with the lemon juice. Season with salt and pepper and tuck 2 dill sprigs in each cavity.

3. Brush the outside of the fish with a little olive oil and lay in an ovenproof dish. Mix the breadcrumbs with the remaining oil and scatter over the fish. Cover with foil and bake in the oven for 20–25 minutes or until the fish is cooked through.

4. Meanwhile, heat the butter in a small pan. Add the garlic and cook until soft but not brown. Add the chanterelles and cook gently until they are tender.

5. Serve the fish and mushrooms with the sour cream drizzled around, garnished with the reserved dill sprigs and lemon wedges.

Preparation time: 10 min
Cooking time: 25 min
Serves 2

2 perch, gutted and heads removed
juice of 1 lemon
salt and pepper to taste
6 sprigs dill
3 tbsp olive oil
5 tbsp breadcrumbs
2 tbsp butter
1 garlic clove
200g chanterelles, halved
4 tbsp sour cream
lemon wedges, to serve

Steamed turbot with white asparagus

1. Place the potatoes and whole garlic cloves in a large pot of salted water. Boil until tender.

2. Meanwhile, peel the tough outer skin from the asparagus stalks. Tie the asparagus into a bunch and lower into boiling salted water in a narrow pan so the stalks boil and the tips steam. Cook for about 15–20 minutes. Remove from the pan, dress with the butter and set aside to keep warm.

3. When the potatoes are cooked, peel them and pass through a potato ricer with the garlic cloves. Add the milk and olive oil, season with salt and pepper and set aside.

4. Place the wine, bay leaves and juniper in the bottom of a steamer. Lay the turbot fillets in the steamer basket. Season the fish with salt, pepper and chilli pepper and steam for 6–8 minutes or until the fish is just cooked through.

5. Serve the fish on the potato and garlic purée with the asparagus alongside.

Preparation time: 15 min
Cooking time: 30 min
Serves 4

250g floury potatoes
4 garlic cloves
1 bunch white asparagus
2 tbsp butter
75ml milk
2 tbsp olive oil
salt and pepper to taste
250ml white wine
2 bay leaves
4 juniper berries
4 fillets turbot
dried chilli pepper

Prawns with ginger and tomato dip in shells

1. Drop the tomatoes into boiling water for 30 seconds. Remove the skin and chop the flesh.

2. Mix the chopped tomatoes with the ginger, garlic, honey, olive oil, lime juice and zest. Season with salt and pepper and set aside.

3. Heat the vegetable oil in a large frying pan and fry the prawns until cooked through. Remove from the pan and add the fish, frying gently until cooked through.

4. Add the tomato salsa to the clam shells. Scatter over the almonds and top with a prawn and a piece of fish.

Preparation time: 15 min
Cooking time: 15 min
Serves 4

4 large tomatoes
thumb sized piece of fresh ginger,
  peeled and finely chopped
1 garlic clove, finely chopped
1 tsp runny honey
2 tbsp olive oil
juice and zest of 1 lime
salt and pepper to taste
3 tbsp vegetable oil
12 king prawns, peeled
200g white fish fillet, cubed
1 tbsp flaked almonds, toasted
12 large clam shells

Tomato, anchovy and cheese pizza

Preparation time: 20 min
 plus 1 h rising
Cooking time: 30 min
Serves 2

For the pizza bases:
450g wholemeal flour
2 sachets easy blend yeast
1 tsp salt
1 tsp sugar
250ml warm water

For the topping:
2 tbsp olive oil
1 onion, finely chopped
1 garlic clove, chopped
450g tomatoes, deseeded and
 flesh chopped
salt and pepper to taste
1 jar anchovies, drained
8 slices mozzarella
handful of baby spinach

1. Mix the ingredients for the pizza bases together to make a dough. You may need to add a little more water. Turn onto a floured board, knead for 5 minutes and return to the bowl. Cover and leave to rise in a warm place for about 1 hour or until the dough has doubled in size.

2. Meanwhile, heat the oil in a pan. Add the onion and gently cook until soft but not brown. Add the garlic and tomatoes and cook for about 10 minutes. Season with salt and pepper.

3. Heat the oven to 210°C (425°F). Turn the dough onto a floured board, knead for about 2 minutes and shape into 2 pizza bases. Place on greased cookie sheets.

4. Spread the tomato mixture onto the pizzas, lay on the anchovies, mozzarella and spinach and bake in the oven for 15–20 minutes.

Roasted bass with provençal vegetables

1. Heat 6 tablespoons of the oil in a large pan and gently cook the onion slices until they start to brown.

2. Add the garlic, fennel, pepper and half the courgette slices, cook gently for 5 minutes then add the tomatoes and the wine. Season with salt and pepper and bring to a simmer.

3. Heat the oven to 180°C (375°F). Pour the sauce into a large ovenproof dish. Season the inside of the fish with salt and pepper and tuck the herbs into the cavity. Lay the fish on top of the sauce and arrange the remaining courgette slices on top.

4. Drizzle with the remaining olive oil, cover and bake in the oven for 25–30 minutes or until the fish is cooked through.

Preparation time: 20 min
Cooking time: 40 min
Serves 2

125ml olive oil
1 onion, finely sliced
2 garlic cloves, chopped
1 fennel bulb, chopped
1 red pepper, deseeded and
* chopped*
2 courgettes, thinly sliced
4 large tomatoes, chopped
250ml white wine
salt and pepper to taste
1 bay leaf
1 sprig thyme
1 sprig rosemary
1 large sea bass, scaled
* and gutted*

Tacos with turbot ceviche and avocado

1. Mix the turbot with about half the lime juice and the crushed garlic. Set aside to marinate for 45 minutes.

2. Heat the taco shells according to the packet instructions. Mix the shallots, avocado, cucumber, vegetable oil and parsley with the remaining lime juice. Season with salt and pepper.

3. Place a few spinach leaves in the tacos and add the turbot ceviche and the avocado mixture.

Preparation time: 10 min
 plus 45 min marinating
Serves 4

600g turbot fillet, sliced
juice of 4 limes
2 garlic cloves, crushed
8 taco shells
2 shallots, finely chopped
2 avocados, peeled, stones removed
 and chopped
1 cucumber, peeled, seeds removed
 and chopped
2 tbsp vegetable oil
1 tbsp chopped parsley
salt and pepper to taste
1 handful baby spinach

Oven-baked sardines

1. Mix together the onion, anchovies, tomatoes, garlic, capers, oregano, basil, parsley and almonds. Mix in the lemon juice and 2 tablespoons of the oil. Season with salt and pepper and set aside.

2. Heat the oven to 200°C (400°F). Wash the courgettes, chop off the ends and cut lengthways into approximately 5mm slices.

3. Brush an ovenproof dish with a little of the oil. Lay in the sliced courgettes, brush with more oil and season with salt and pepper.

4. Wash and scale the sardines. Chop off the heads, slice along the underside of the belly and remove the guts and backbones. Wash again, pat dry with kitchen paper and season with pepper.

5. Open up the sardines and lay on top of the courgettes, skin-side up. Spread the onion mixture over the sardines, cover the dish with tin foil and bake in the oven for about 20 minutes or until the fish are cooked through.

Preparation time: 30 min
Cooking time: 20 min
Serves 4

1 onion, finely chopped
2 anchovy fillets, finely
  chopped
8 sun-dried tomatoes, finely
  chopped
4 garlic cloves, roughly
  chopped
1 tbsp capers, chopped
2 tbsp chopped oregano
2 tbsp chopped basil
2 tbsp chopped parsley
50g chopped almonds
juice of 1 lemon
salt and pepper to taste
4 tbsp olive oil
4 small courgettes
700g fresh sardines

Fish dumplings in spinach cream sauce

1. Place the fish, bread, lemon juice and half the lemon zest in a food processor with the egg white and half of the cream. Blend to make a smooth purée, season with salt and pepper and place in the refrigerator.

2. Heat the butter in a large pan. Add the spring onions and gently cook until soft but not brown. Add the spinach and stir for 1 minute. Add the wine and fish stock. Bring to a simmer, cook gently for 5 minutes and set aside.

3. Bring a large pot of water to the boil and add 1 teaspoon of salt. Shape the fish mixture into 8 dumplings and drop into the boiling water – you will probably have to cook the dumplings in batches. Simmer gently for 8–10 minutes then remove with a slotted spoon and set aside.

4. Return the spinach pan to the heat, add the remaining cream and bring to a simmer. Mix the cornflour with a little water and add to the pan with the dumplings. Season with salt and pepper and serve garnished with the reserved lemon zest.

Preparation time: 10 min
Cooking time: 25 min
Serves 4

*500g white fish fillet, boned
removed and flesh chopped
4 slices white bread, crusts
removed and roughly torn
juice and zest of 1 lemons
1 egg white
250ml double cream
salt and pepper to taste
2 tbsp butter
8 spring onions, finely chopped
250g spinach, washed and
chopped
125ml dry white wine
250ml fish stock
1 tbsp cornflour*

Sea bass with king prawns on egg noodles

1. Cook the egg noodles according to the packet instructions. Drain well and set aside.

2. Meanwhile, sprinkle the sea bass with a little salt. Heat the vegetable oil in a large frying pan and add the sea bass, skin-side down. Cook for 2–3 minutes then turn over and cook for a further 3 minutes or until the fish is just cooked through. Remove from the pan and set aside in a warm place.

3. Add the prawns to the pan and quickly fry until cooked through. Set aside.

4. Wipe the pan clean and add the sesame oil. When hot, add the red and green chillies. Fry briefly, then add the spring onions. Cook for 2 minutes then add the drained noodles and the lime juice. Stir to heat through.

5. Pile onto plates, top with the sea bass and prawns and dot the chilli sauce around. Serve garnished with thyme sprigs.

Preparation time: 15 min
Cooking time: 15 min
Serves 4

300g egg noodles
4 sea bass fillets
3 tsp vegetable oil
8 king prawns, peeled
3 tbsp sesame oil
2 red chilli peppers, deseeded and sliced
2 green chilli peppers, deseeded and sliced
8 spring onions, sliced
juice of 2 limes
1 tbsp chilli sauce
thyme sprigs, to serve

Asian-style trout in greaseproof paper

Preparation time: 15 min
Cooking time: 35 min
Serves 4

4 fresh trout, gutted and scaled
salt and pepper to taste
6 spring onions
3 tbsp vegetable oil
2 garlic cloves, chopped
thumb size piece fresh ginger,
  peeled and chopped
1 stalk lemongrass, outer skin
  removed and finely chopped
2 red chilli peppers, deseeded
  and chopped
8 sugar snap peas, halved
2 carrots, cut into very fine strips
1 tbsp sesame oil
juice of 1 lime
2 tbsp soy sauce
1 tbsp dry sherry

1. Heat the oven to 180°C (350°F).

2. Wash the fish and pat dry with kitchen paper. Season the cavities with salt and pepper.

3. Finely slice the white parts of the spring onions and shred the green parts into long strips.

4. Heat the vegetable oil in a large pan. Gently add the white parts of the spring onions, garlic, ginger, lemongrass and chilli peppers. Fry until they are soft.

5. Lightly oil 4 large sheets of greaseproof paper and place a fish in the middle of each. Place the fish in a large roasting pan, drawing up the edges of the greaseproof paper.

6. Place the spring onion mixture in the cavities of the fish and spread the sugar snaps, carrot and green parts of the spring onions on top.

7. Mix together the sesame oil, lime juice, soy sauce and sherry and pour over the fish. Scrunch the edges of the paper together to make a seal and bake in the oven for 25–30 minutes or until the fish are cooked through. Baste the fish with the cooking juices before serving.

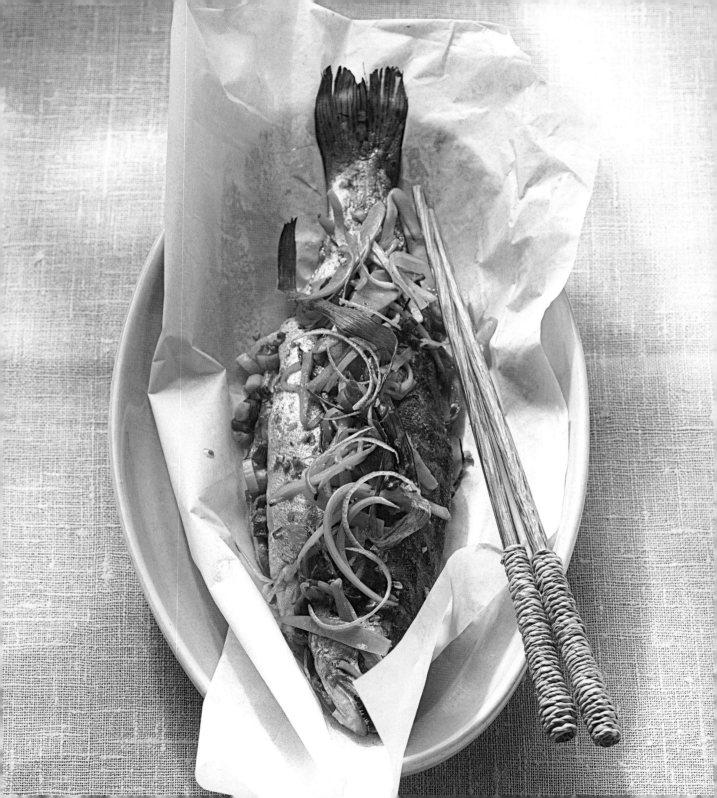

Salmon strudel

1. Heat oven to 200°C (400°F). Cut the kohl rabi into 5mm slices and blanch in boiling water for 3 minutes. Cut the stalks from the cabbage leaves and blanch in boiling water for 30 seconds. Drain well and pat dry with paper. Blend the trout and cream in a food processor until smooth. Whisk the eggs until fluffy and fold in the trout mixture. Season and set aside. Cut the salmon fillet into 3cm strips.

2. Brush the filo pastry sheets with melted butter and lay one on top of the other in a large roasting pan. Lay the cabbage leaves along the pastry, overlapping them as you go. Pour over one-third of the trout mixture along the middle of the cabbage leaves. Lay on some of the kohl rabi slices then lay strips of salmon. Top with the remaining kohl rabi slices and pour the remaining trout mix over it.

3. Roll the cabbage leaves to make a tight parcel, taking care that the filling doesn't spill onto the pastry, and tuck in the edges. Roll the pastry around the cabbage parcel, moistening the edges to seal, and brush with the remaining melted butter. Place the roasting pan in the oven and bake for 30 minutes, until golden brown.

4. To make the sauce: heat the butter and add the shallot. Cook until soft, but not brown. Add the white wine and boil until reduced by half. Add the cream, bring to a boil and purée with a hand blender. Pass through a fine sieve into a clean pan. Season with salt and white pepper and keep warm.

5. To make the tomato garnish: use a sharp knife to peel away the skin from each tomato in one continuous piece. Roll each piece up to make a rose shape and set aside.

6. Sprinkle the chives around the rims of the plates. Pour the sauce onto each plate. Place a piece of strudel in the middle and garnish with a tomato rose.

Preparation time: 30 min
Cooking time: 45 min
Serves 4

For the strudel:
2 medium kohl rabi, peeled
4 cabbage leaves
250g trout fillet, chopped
100ml double cream
2 eggs
500g salmon fillet, skinned
4 sheets filo pastry
4 tbsp butter, melted

For the sauce:
2 tbsp butter
1 shallot, chopped
150ml dry white wine
100ml double cream
4 tomatoes, to serve
4 tbsp chopped chives, to serve

Baked halibut steak on chickpeas

1. Boil the potatoes in salted water until tender. Mash with the butter and horseradish cream and set aside.

2. Heat the oven 200°C (400°F). Wash the halibut steaks and pat dry with kitchen paper. Sprinkle with the lemon juice and oil, season with salt and pepper and bake in the oven for 10–15 minutes or until the fish is cooked through.

3. Meanwhile, heat the butter in a large pan. Add the garlic and chilli and gently cook until soft. Add the wine, let bubble then add the spinach and chickpeas. Cover the pan with a lid and cook for 3–4 minutes or until the spinach has wilted.

4. Serve the fish on a bed of the spinach and chickpeas topped with a little mashed potato. Season with salt and pepper and garnish with a pinch of ground pink pepper and the coriander.

Preparation time: 10 min
Cooking time: 30 min
Serves 4

For the potato garnish:
2 large potatoes, peeled and
  chopped
1 tbsp butter
1 tbsp horseradish cream

For the halibut:
4 halibut steaks
2 tbsp lemon juice
2 tbsp olive oil
salt and pepper to taste
coriander leaves, to serve
ground pink peppercorns, to
  serve

For the chickpeas:
3 tbsp butter
1 garlic clove, finely chopped
1 red chilli pepper, deseeded
  and finely chopped
125ml white wine
450g spinach, washed
400g tinned chickpeas, drained
  and rinsed

Kedgeree

1. Cook the rice according to the packet instructions.

2. Meanwhile, put the eggs into a pan of boiling water and cook for 7 minutes, then hold under cold running water to cool completely and peel off the shells.

3. Put the haddock and bay leaves in a shallow pan with enough water to cover. Bring to the boil, cover and simmer for about 5 minutes or until the fish is cooked through.

4. Remove the fish from pan and let cool. Remove the skin from fish, flake the flesh into chunks and set aside.

5. Melt the butter in a pan over a low heat. Add the onion and cook until soft but not brown. Add the ginger and garlic, cook for 2 minutes, then add the curry powder.

6. Cook for a further 2 minutes, then add the spring onions and lemon juice.

7. Add the fish, rice and parsley to the pan, stirring gently, season with salt and pepper and heat through.

8. Quarter the eggs and serve on top of the kedgeree. Garnish with the lemon halves.

Preparation time: 10 min
Cooking time: 30 min
Serves 4

200g long grain rice
4 eggs
450g undyed smoked haddock fillets
2 bay leaves
50g butter
1 onion, finely chopped
thumb size piece fresh ginger, peeled and grated
1 garlic clove, crushed
2 tbsp curry powder
4 spring onions, finely sliced
juice of 1 lemon
2 tbsp chopped parsley
salt and pepper to taste

To garnish:
2 lemons, halved

Summery octopus salad

Preparation time: 30 min
Cooking time: 3 h
Serves 4

1 large octopus, cleaned
250ml white wine
2 bay leaves
1 sprig thyme
6 peppercorns
125ml olive oil
juice of 1 lemon
2 tbsp chopped parsley
1 onion, finely sliced into rings
12 cherry tomatoes, halved
12 black olives
1 tbsp chopped basil
salt and pepper to taste
lettuce leaves, to serve
basil sprigs, to serve

1. Heat the oven to 180°C (350°F).

2. Bring a large pan of salted water to a boil and blanch the octopus for 2 minutes. Drain, remove the head and chop the tentacles into large chunks.

3. Place the chopped tentacles in an ovenproof pot with the wine, bay leaves, thyme and peppercorns. Cover with a tightly fitting lid and place in the oven for about 3 hours or until the octopus is tender. Check the pot from time to time, baste the tentacles and add a little water if they are becoming dry.

4. Drain the octopus, discarding the herbs and peppercorns. Mix together the oil, lemon juice and parsley and mix in the octopus while still warm.

5. Let cool and mix in the onion, tomatoes, olives and basil. Season with salt and pepper and serve garnished with the lettuce leaves and basil sprigs.

Crab ravioli with fresh chives

1. Mix the ingredients for the pasta together and knead to make a dough. Wrap in cling film and chill for 30 minutes.

2. To make the filling: mix together the ingredients for the filling, season with salt and pepper and set aside.

3. To make the sauce: Heat the oil and butter in a small pan and add the saffron threads. Set aside to infuse while you make the ravioli.

4. Roll the dough out as thinly as possible and cut 24 circles, each slightly larger than 10cm in diameter. Place a spoonful of the filling in the middle of half the pasta circles and moisten the edges with a little water. Top with the remaining pasta circles and seal tightly by pressing with your fingers.

5. Use a 10cm cutter to trim the edges off each of the ravioli. Bring a large pan of salted water to a boil and simmer the ravioli for about 5 minutes. Remove from the pan with a slotted spoon and keep warm.

6. Lay the chives onto serving dishes and top with the ravioli. Quickly reheat the sauce, stir in the lemon zest and chopped chives. Season with salt and pepper. Drizzle the sauce over the ravioli and serve immediately.

Preparation time: 45 min
  plus 1 h chilling
Cooking time: 10 min
Serves 4

For the pasta:
350g pasta flour
50g semolina
3 eggs
2 egg yolks
½ tsp salt

For the filling:
100g mascarpone
zest of 1 lemon
250g white crabmeat
25g fresh breadcrumbs
2 eggs
2 tbsp semolina
salt and pepper to taste

For the sauce:
2 tbsp olive oil
3 tbsp butter
pinch of saffron strands
zest of 1 lemon
2 tbsp chopped chives
large bunch of chives, to serve

Grilled monkfish wrapped in pancetta

1. Heat the grill to its highest setting.

2. Season the monkfish with salt and pepper and wrap in the pancetta, securing with cocktail sticks or kitchen string.

3. Place under the grill and cook for 10–15 minutes, turning frequently, or until the fish is cooked through.

4. Mix together the oil, lemon juice and capers. Season with salt and pepper and set aside.

5. Serve the fish on a bed of rocket with the dressing drizzled over.

Preparation time: 15 min
Cooking time: 15 min
Serves 4

4 pieces monkfish fillet (each about 175g)
salt and pepper to taste
8 slices pancetta, thinly sliced
4 tbsp olive oil
2 tbsp lemon juice
2 tbsp capers, drained and rinsed
1 bunch rocket

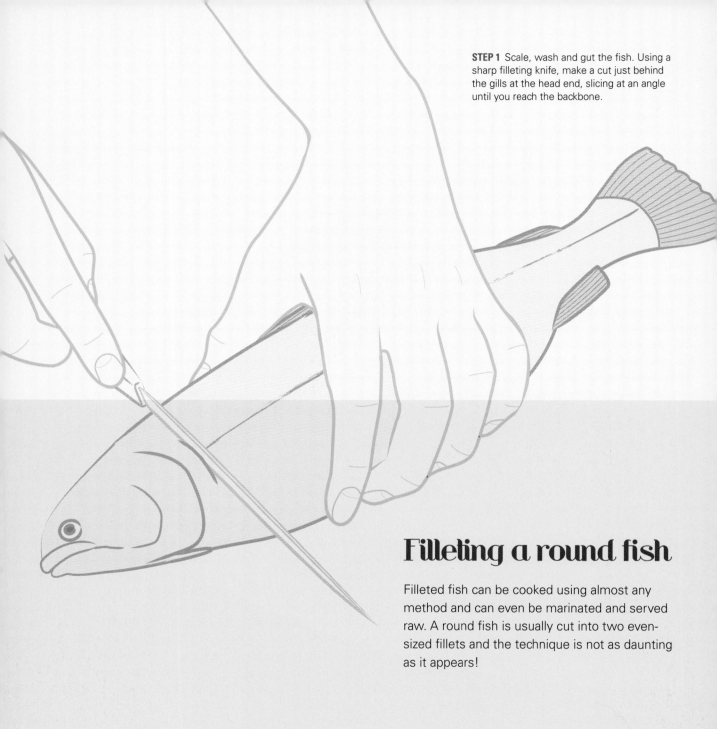

STEP 1 Scale, wash and gut the fish. Using a sharp filleting knife, make a cut just behind the gills at the head end, slicing at an angle until you reach the backbone.

Filleting a round fish

Filleted fish can be cooked using almost any method and can even be marinated and served raw. A round fish is usually cut into two even-sized fillets and the technique is not as daunting as it appears!

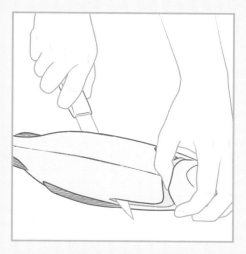

STEP 2 Starting at the head end, near the gills, cut the fish all along the length of the top side of the backbone, keeping the blade horizontal.

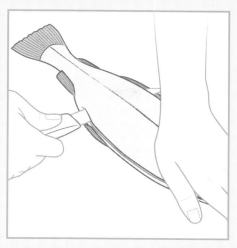

STEP 3 Once the whole blade of the knife is underneath the fillet, place your palm on the skin to hold it firm and cut away the fillet down to the tail.

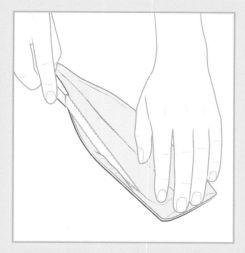

STEP 4 Repeat on the other side then place the two fillets on a chopping board. Trim away any bones or excess skin along the edges of the fillets.

STEP 5 Place the fillet skin-side down on a board. Holding the tail with one hand, insert the knife at the tail and cut away the flesh, close to the skin.

Grilled fish kebabs with orange and ginger on couscous

1. Marinate the tuna with the ginger, oil, orange zest and the honey. Refrigerate for 30 minutes.

2. Meanwhile, mix the raisins with the orange juice and zest. Set aside.

3. Cook the couscous according to the package instructions.

4. Fluff the couscous up with a fork and mix in the soaked raisins, carrot, olive oil, almonds and parsley. Season with salt and pepper and set aside.

5. Thread the tuna cubes onto wooden skewers, reserving the marinade.

6. Heat an oiled griddle pan or grill. Cook the fish skewers for 5–6 minutes, turning frequently, or until the fish is just cooked through. Place the skewers on a serving plate with the couscous alongside.

7. Place the marinade in small pan. Bring to a boil, then drizzle over the skewers. Serve garnished with the orange slices.

Preparation time: 20 min
  plus 30 min marinating
Cooking time: 15 min
Serves 4

600g tuna fillet, cut into cubes
thumb-size piece fresh ginger,
  peeled and grated
2 tbsp olive oil
zest and juice of 1 orange
2 tbsp honey

For the couscous:
3 tbsp raisins
zest and juice of 1 orange
250g couscous
1 carrot, peeled and grated
2 tbsp olive oil
3 tbsp flaked almonds, toasted
3 sprigs parsley, roughly chopped
salt and pepper to taste
orange slices, to serve

Grilled lemon and garlic prawns with rice

1. Marinate the prawns with the lemon juice and zest, garlic, cumin seeds and 2 tablespoons of the oil. Set aside for 30 minutes.

2. Meanwhile, cook the rice according to the packet instructions. Set aside and keep warm.

3. Thread the prawns onto wooden skewers. Heat the remaining oil in a large frying pan. Add the prawn skewers and cook gently for about 2 minutes on both sides or until the prawns are cooked through.

4. Serve the skewers on a bed of rice garnished with the lemon slices.

Preparation time: 10 min
  plus 30 min marinating
Cooking time: 15 min
Serves 4

32 king prawns, peeled
juice and zest of 2 lemons
2 garlic cloves, finely chopped
1 tsp cumin seeds
4 tbsp olive oil
200g long grain rice
lemon slices, to serve

Coley fried in batter with apple remoulade

1. To make the remoulade: mix all the ingredients together. Season with salt and pepper and set aside.

2. To make the coley: wash the fish and pat dry with kitchen paper. Mix the flour and lager, seasoning with salt and pepper. The batter should be thick enough to coat the back of a wooden spoon.

3. Heat the oil in a deep pan to 180°C (350°F). If it is hot enough, bubbles will appear on a wooden spoon dipped into it.

4. Coat the fish pieces in the batter and deep-fry in the oil for about 6–8 minutes or until golden brown and crisp. Drain on kitchen paper and serve immediately with the remoulade.

Preparation time: 20 min
Cooking time: 10 min
Serves 4

For the remoulade:
1 red onion, finely chopped
2 dessert apples, peeled, cored and chopped
1 carrot, peeled and grated
juice of 1 lemon
5 tbsp mayonnaise
2 tbsp chopped parsley
salt and pepper to taste

For the coley:
750g coley fillet, cut into large pieces
225g self-raising flour
300ml cold lager
sunflower oil, for deep-frying

Spaghetti vongole

Preparation time: 10 min
Cooking time: 15 min
Serves 4

400g spaghetti
2 tbsp butter
1 tbsp olive oil
1 shallot, very finely chopped
2 garlic cloves, finely chopped
1kg clams, cleaned
125ml white wine
2 tbsp chopped parsley
salt and pepper to taste

1. Bring a large pan of salted water to the boil and cook the spaghetti for 10–12 minutes or until tender.

2. Meanwhile, heat the butter and oil in a large pan. Add the shallot and garlic, and gently cook until soft but not brown.

3. Add the clams and the wine, cover with a lid and cook for 2–3 minutes or until the clams have opened.

4. Drain the spaghetti and add it to the clam pan with the parsley. Stir well, season with salt and pepper and serve immediately.

Plaice with lemon

1. Heat the butter in a large frying pan until it begins to foam. Add the plaice, season with salt and pepper and cook gently for 4 minutes or until the fish is starting to brown, basting from time to time. Carefully turn over and cook for another 2 minutes.

2. Pour over the wine, let it bubble then add the lemon juice and chopped parsley.

3. Serve the plaice on warmed serving plates garnished with the parsley sprigs and lemon wedges.

Preparation time: 10 min
Cooking time: 10 min
Serves 2

25g butter
2 small plaice, trimmed with
* heads and dark skin removed*
1 tbsp white wine
salt and pepper to taste
juice of 1 lemon
1 tbsp chopped parsley
parsley sprigs, to serve
lemon wedges, to serve

Battered plaice with potatoes and tartare sauce

1. To make the tartare sauce: mix together the ingredients, season with salt and pepper and set aside.

2. To make the potatoes, boil them in a large pan of salted water until they are tender. Drain, then return to the pan with the butter and chopped parsley, mix gently and set aside in a warm place.

3. Meanwhile, wash the plaice fillets and pat dry on the kitchen paper.

4. Mix together the self-raising flour, egg and cold lager to make a thick batter. Season with salt and pepper and set aside.

5. Heat the oil in a deep pan. When bubbles appear on a wooden spoon dipped in the oil, it is hot enough.

6. Dredge the fish in the flour. Dip into the batter, ensuring it is evenly coated, and deep-fry, one fillet at a time, for 6–8 minutes or until the fish is golden brown and crisp. Drain on kitchen paper and set aside in a warm place while you cook the remaining fish.

7. Serve the fish garnished with lemon wedges and the buttered potatoes and tartare sauce alongside.

Preparation time: 15 min
Cooking time: 35 min
Serves 4

For the tartare sauce:
250ml mayonnaise
3 tbsp capers, chopped
2 shallots, finely chopped
1 tbsp lemon juice
salt and pepper to taste

For the potatoes:
600g new potatoes, scrubbed
25g butter
1 tbsp chopped parsley

For the fish:
4 plaice fillets
225g self-raising flour
1 egg
200ml cold lager
vegetable oil, for deep-frying
flour, for dredging
lemon wedges, to serve

Grilled sole

1. Heat the grill to its highest setting.

2. Wash the soles and pat dry with kitchen paper. Rub with the lemon juice and season with salt and pepper.

3. Brush the fish with a little oil and grill for 3–4 minutes on each side or until just cooked through. Serve garnished with lemon slices and parsley.

Preparation time: 5 min
Cooking time: 10 min
Serves 2

2 large sole
juice of 1 lemon
salt and pepper to taste
2 tbsp olive oil
lemon slices, to serve
parsley leaves, to serve

Grilled swordfish with pineapple salsa

Preparation time: 10 min
Cooking time: 10 min
Serves 4

1 small pineapple, peeled, core
  removed and flesh chopped
½ red pepper, deseeded and finely
  chopped
½ green pepper, deseeded and
  finely chopped
1 red onion, finely chopped
2 tbsp chopped coriander leaves,
  plus extra to serve
2 tbsp lime juice
3 tbsp olive oil
salt and pepper to taste
4 swordfish steaks
1 tbsp lime juice
3 tbsp olive oil

1. Mix the chopped pineapple, peppers, onion and chopped coriander with 1 tablespoon of the lime juice and a few drops of the oil. Season with salt and pepper and set aside.

2. Brush the swordfish steaks with the remaining lime juice and season with salt and pepper. Heat the remaining oil in a griddle pan and add the fish. Cook for 3–4 minutes on each side or until cooked through.

3. Serve the fish with the pineapple salsa, garnished with the coriander leaves.

Farfalle with king prawns and artichokes

1. Cook the farfalle in a large pan of boiling salted water for 12 minutes or until ready to serve.

2. Meanwhile, trim the artichokes, remove the outer leaves and chop into quarters vertically. Plunge into cold water with a teaspoon of the lemon juice to prevent discolouring.

3. Heat the oil in a wide pan and gently cook the garlic and bacon until lightly browned. Add the pepper, cook for 2 more minutes then add the wine and the drained artichokes.

4. Cover with a lid and simmer for 10 minutes. Remove the lid and simmer until most of the liquid has evapourated.

5. Add the prawns and fry until lightly browned and cooked through.

6. Drain the farfalle and mix into the prawns with the olive oil and remaining lemon juice. Season with salt and pepper and serve immediately.

Preparation time: 10 min
Cooking time: 25 min
Serves 4

400g farfalle
4 baby artichokes, trimmed
juice of 1 lemon
2 tbsp vegetable oil
1 garlic clove, finely chopped
100g bacon, chopped
½ red pepper, deseeded and
  roughly chopped
125ml white wine
12 king prawns, peeled
3 tbsp olive oil
salt and pepper to taste

Halibut on a bed of risotto

1. Heat the butter in a wide pan. Add the shallot and garlic, and gently cook until soft but not brown.

2. Add the rice, stir to coat with the butter, then add the wine and let bubble. Add a ladle of the stock, stir until it has been absorbed by the rice then add the rest of the stock, one ladle at a time until the rice is just cooked through. Add a little more stock or water if necessary. This will take about 25 minutes; you should stir the risotto continuously as it cooks.

3. Remove the pan from the heat, stir in the Parmesan, marjoram leaves, lemon juice and olive oil and keep warm while you cook the rest of the dish.

4. Drop the tomatoes into boiling water for 30 seconds, then refresh under cold running water, remove the skins and seeds and finely chop the flesh. Set aside.

5. Wash the fish, pat dry with kitchen paper and season with salt and pepper. Heat the butter in a clean frying pan until it begins to foam. Add the fish and cook for 3–4 minutes on each side or until the fish is just cooked through. Remove the fish from the pan and keep warm.

6. Wipe the pan clean with kitchen paper and heat the oil gently. Add the onion, cook gently for 2 minutes, then add the tomatoes and cook for 1 more minute.

7. Spoon the risotto onto warmed serving plates, add the fish and top with the onion and tomato mixture. Garnish with mixed micro herbs.

Preparation time: 15 min
Cooking time: 35 min
Serves 4

4 tomatoes
4 pieces halibut fillet
2 tbsp butter
2 tbsp olive oil
1 small red onion, finely chopped
mixed micro herbs, to serve

For the risotto:
2 tbsp butter
1 shallot
1 garlic clove
200g risotto rice
100ml dry white wine
800ml vegetable stock, hot
100g Parmesan
1 tbsp marjoram leaves
juice of 1 lemon
1 tbsp olive oil
salt and pepper to taste

STEP 1 Rub off the scales, wash the fish, then pat dry. Using a filleting knife, slit the stomach from the head to the tail. Remove the guts with your fingers. Wash out the cavity well.

Preparing a whole fish

You can buy fish ready prepared, but it's cheaper and pretty easy to do the work yourself. A whole fish needs scaling and gutting before cooking, and you can fillet them too if you wish. None of these jobs are difficult or time-consuming.

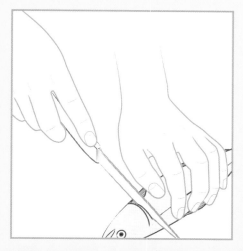

STEP 2 Hold the body of the fish firmly with your fingertips and, using a sharp kitchen knife, make a cut below the gills, slicing right through the backbone.

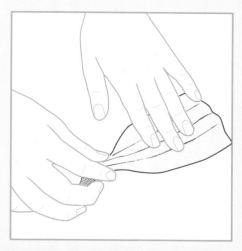

STEP 3 Open out the fish along the slit stomach and place it, flesh-side down, on a board. Press firmly along the backbone until the fish lies flat.

STEP 4 Turn the fish over onto the skin side and carefully pull away the backbone using your fingers. Remove any remaining bones with tweezers.

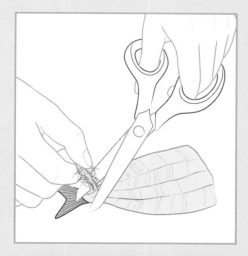

STEP 5 To remove the backbone completely, pull it towards you and, using sharp kitchen scissors, snip through the backbone close to the tail.

Barbecued squid with butter sauce and parsley

1. Marinate the squid with the lemon juice in a bowl, ensuring that the squid is thoroughly coated. Set aside to marinate for 30 minutes.

2. Heat the barbecue or a grill to its highest setting and cook the squid, reserving its marinade, for about 3 minutes on each side.

3. Meanwhile, melt the butter in a wide pan and add the squid marinade and parsley. Bring to a simmer and season with salt and pepper. Pour the sauce over the squid and serve immediately.

Preparation time: 10 min
plus 30 min marinating
Cooking time: 10 min
Serves 4

8 medium squid, cleaned
juice of 2 lemons
75g butter
3 tbsp chopped parsley
salt and pepper to taste

Swordfish and vegetable kebabs with herb sauce

1. For the sauce, place all the ingredients in a food processor or blender and pulse to form a paste. Season with salt and pepper and set aside.

2. Heat an oiled griddle pan. Thread wooden skewers with the swordfish, onion, tomatoes, pepper and caper berries. Brush with the oil and cook in the pan for 6–8 minutes, turning frequently, or until the fish is cooked through.

3. Serve the kebabs drizzled with the herb sauce.

Preparation time: 15 min
Cooking time: 10 min
Serves 4

For the sauce:
1 handful fresh mint leaves
1 handful fresh parsley leaves
1 handful fresh basil leaves
juice of 1 lemon
100ml olive oil
1 tbsp capers
1 garlic clove
salt and pepper to taste

For the kebabs:
450g swordfish fillet, cut into chunks
1 red onion, cut into wedges
8 cherry tomatoes
½ yellow pepper, deseeded and cut into chunks
8 caper berries
2 tbsp olive oil

King prawn and pumpkin curry

1. Heat the oil in a large pan and gently cook the shallot, garlic and ginger until soft but not brown.

2. Stir in the curry paste then add the pumpkin and pour over the stock. Bring to a simmer then add the coconut milk and simmer gently for 15 minutes or until the pumpkin is nearly tender.

3. Add the prawns, lime juice, fish sauce and sugar and cook gently until the prawns are cooked through.

4. Serve with the spring onions scattered over.

Preparation time: 10 min
Cooking time: 25 min
Serves 4

4 tbsp vegetable oil
1 shallot, roughly chopped
2 garlic cloves, peeled
*thumb size piece fresh ginger,
    peeled and grated*
2 tbsp yellow curry paste
*1 small pumpkin, deseeded, seeds
    removed and flesh chopped*
500ml vegetable stock
400ml coconut milk
24 king prawns, peeled
juice of 1 lime
2 tbsp fish sauce
1 tsp sugar
4 spring onions, sliced, to serve

Trout veronique with grape sauce and broccoli

Preparation time: 15 min
Cooking time: 25 min
Serves 4

2 tbsp butter
4 trout, gutted
125ml white wine
125ml fish stock or water
250g broccoli
200g white grapes
250ml double cream
salt and pepper to taste
2 tbsp parsley, very finely
   chopped

1. Heat the oven to 200°C (400°F).

2. Use the butter to liberally grease a roasting pan large enough to hold all the fish. Lay the fish in the pan, pour over the wine and stock and cover with a tin foil. Place the pan in the oven and cook for 10–15 minutes or until the fish is cooked through.

3. Meanwhile, boil or steam the broccoli for 4–5 minutes or until tender. Drain well and set aside in a warm place.

4. Place the grapes in a small bowl, pour over boiling water and let stand for 1 minute. Drain well, then peel off the skins, slice the grapes in half and remove the seeds.

5. When the fish is cooked, remove from the pan and carefully peel off the skin. Remove the fillets from the bone using a sharp knife and set the fillets aside in a warm place.

6. Strain the cooking liquid from the fish pan into a small saucepan. Bring to a boil, let it reduce a little, then add the cream. Simmer for 5 minutes over a very gentle heat, then season with salt and pepper.

7. Place two fish fillets one on top of the other onto each serving plate. Scatter the parsley along the length of the fish and serve with the broccoli, grapes and cream sauce.

Ceviche – fish fillet with coriander and tomatoes

1. Place the fish in a deep bowl and add the spring onions, lemon juice, chillies and 1 teaspoon salt. Cover and place in the fridge for 3 hours.

2. Add the tomatoes into the mixture. Serve with the mixture spooned over the fish and the coriander to garnish.

Preparation time: 10 min
  plus 3 h marinating
Serves 4

600g sea bass fillet, cubed
2 spring onions, very finely
  chopped
juice of 2 lemons
2 green chilli peppers, deseeded
  and finely chopped
2 large tomatoes, skinned,
  deseeded and finely diced
coriander leaves, to serve

Sea bass fillet with a herb and garlic crust

1. Heat the oil in a large frying pan. Add the garlic and chopped pepper, and gently cook until soft.

2. Add the breadcrumbs, cook until lightly browned and crisp then stir in the parsley, thyme, olives and lemon juice. Season with salt and pepper, remove from the pan and set aside.

3. Wipe the pan clean with kitchen paper. Heat the butter over a gentle heat and add the fish fillets to the pan.

4. Pour over the wine and stock, bring to a simmer then cover with a lid or tin foil and poach gently for 10 minutes or until the fish is cooked through.

5. Remove the fish from the pan with a slotted spoon and place on serving plates. Spoon over the herb crust and serve garnished with the lettuce and lemon wedges.

Preparation time: 10 min
Cooking time: 20 min
Serves 4

4 tbsp olive oil
2 garlic cloves, finely chopped
1 red pepper, deseeded and finely chopped
100g fresh breadcrumbs
1 tbsp chopped parsley
1 tbsp chopped thyme
50g black olives, pitted and finely chopped
juice of 1 lemon
salt and pepper to taste
1 tbsp butter
4 fillets sea bass, skinned
125ml white wine
125ml fish stock or water
lettuce, to serve
lemon wedges, to serve

Monkfish fillets with cherry tomatoes and olives

1. Heat 2 tablespoons of oil in a small pan. Add the red pepper and gently cook until soft. Season with salt and pepper, pass through a fine sieve and set aside.

2. Repeat this process with the yellow pepper.

3. Heat the oven to 200°C (400°F). Heat a little more oil in an ovenproof frying pan. Add the garlic and chilli and gently cook for 2 minutes.

4. Add the fish to the pan, lightly sear on all sides then pour over the wine and season with salt and freshly ground black pepper.

5. Add the sage and tomatoes to the pan, baste in the juices then place the pan in the oven and roast for 10–15 minutes or until the fish is coked through. Baste the fish twice during the cooking.

6. Squeeze the lemon juice over the fish and serve on warmed plates with the olives alongside and the lemon juice squeezed over.

Preparation time: 10 min
Cooking time: 25 min
Serves 4

oil, for frying
1 red pepper, deseeded and
  chopped
salt and pepper to taste
1 yellow pepper, deseeded and
  chopped
2 garlic cloves, finely chopped
2 red chilli peppers, deseeded and
  finely chopped
800g monkfish, cut into large
  pieces
125ml white wine
2 tbsp sage leaves, roughly
  chopped
12 cherry tomatoes
juice of 1 lemon, to serve
8 black olives, to serve

Seared sea bass with oriental noodle salad and sweet chilli dressing

Preparation time: 15 min
Cooking time: 5 min
Serves 4

4 sea bass fillets
salt and pepper to taste
noodle salad
125g ramen noodles
1 mango, stoned, peeled and sliced
75g beansprouts
2 spring onions, shredded
1 carrot, finely shredded
1 red chilli, seeded and sliced
50g coriander leaves
2 tbsp cashew nuts, toasted and
   chopped
1 tbsp toasted sesame seed

For the dressing:
4 tbsp rice wine vinegar
3 tbsp sesame oil
4 tbsp sweet chilli sauce
lemon wedges, to serve

1. Season the sea bass with a little salt and pepper.

2. Place the noodles in a saucepan of boiling water stir and allow to stand for 4 minutes or until tender. Drain and keep warm.

3. Meanwhile, combine the remaining ingredients for the salad and set aside.

4. Combine the ingredients for the dressing.

5. Heat a griddle pan until very hot and quickly sear the sea bass fillet over a high heat for 2 minutes each side, turning once.

6. Toss the noodles with the salad ingredients. Pour about half of the chilli dressing over the salad and toss to coat. Pile onto serving plates. Arrange the fillets on top of the noodle salad, then drizzle the remaining dressing over the top. Serve immediately with lemon wedges for squeezing over the fish and salad.

Mackerel en papillote with orange and mustard

1. Heat the oven to 180°C (350°F). Slash the skin of the mackerel two or three times on each side.

2. Finely grate the zest from one of the oranges, squeeze the juice and mix the juice, zest and mustard together to form a paste. Peel and slice the remaining oranges.

3. Divide the orange slices between four large sheets of non-stick baking parchment. Brush the mustard and orange paste all over the skin of each fish and place on top of the orange slices. Drizzle any remaining paste over the top.

4. Fold up each piece of baking parchment to completely enclose the mackerel and place on a baking sheet. Bake for 15 minutes until the fish flakes easily. Serve in the paper parcels with boiled new potatoes and a fresh green vegetable.

Preparation time: 15 min
Cooking time: 15 min
Serves 4

4 mackerel, cleaned and heads
  removed
3 oranges
3 tbsp wholegrain mustard
boiled new potatoes and green
  vegetables, to serve

Roast halibut with roast new potatoes and peppers

1. Heat the oven to 200°C (400°F). Place the potatoes in a large roasting tin, drizzle with 2 tablespoons olive oil and toss to coat. Roast for 20 minutes.

2. Add the peppers, courgettes, tomatoes and garlic. Toss with the potatoes in the tin. Rub the remaining oil into the fish fillets and season with salt and pepper, and place on top of the part-roasted vegetables. Add the thyme.

3. Return to the oven and roast for 20 minutes until the fish is cooked through and the vegetables are tender.

Preparation time: 20 min
Cooking time: 40 min
Serves 2

450g small new potatoes
3 tbsp olive oil
1 red peppers, seeded and cut into chunks
1 yellow peppers, seeded and cut into chucks
1 courgettes, thickly sliced
3 plum tomatoes, quartered
4 garlic cloves, sliced
2 halibut steaks
salt and pepper to taste
few sprigs of fresh thyme

Index